S0-BRJ-818

THIS
BOOK
BELONGS TO
Arpita
Bose

10/06
27

EYEWITNESS ART

LOOKING AT PAINTINGS

Sandro Botticelli,
Adoration of the Kings, c.1470–75

Agnolo Bronzino, *An Allegory with Venus and Cupid*, c.1545

Bronzino's
Venus and Cupid

Bronzino's *Venus and Cupid* with later overpainting

Tintoretto, *St. George and the Dragon*, c.1560

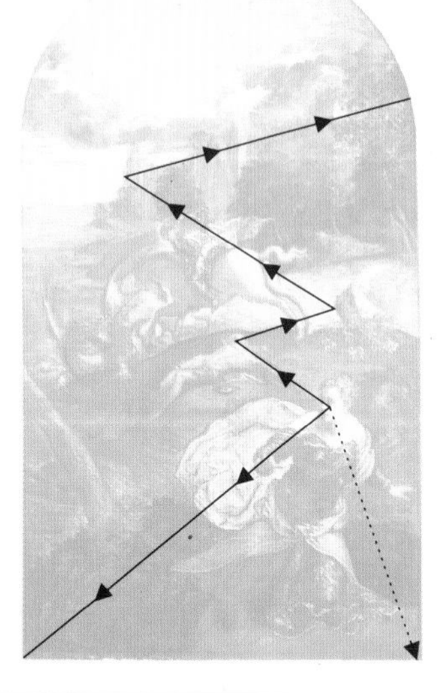

Tintoretto's diagonal composition structure

Paul Cézanne,
Mont Sainte–Victoire, 1904–06

EYEWITNESS ART

LOOKING AT PAINTINGS

JUDE WELTON

Nicholas Hilliard, *Alice Hilliard*, 1578

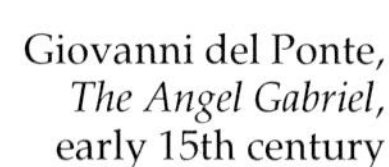

Giovanni del Ponte, *The Angel Gabriel*, early 15th century

Alesso Baldovinetti, *Portrait of a Lady in Yellow*, c.1465

Correggio, *Jupiter and Io*, c.1530

Follower of Fra Angelico, *The Rape of Helen by Paris*, c.1450

IN ASSOCIATION WITH
THE NATIONAL GALLERY LONDON

Duccio, *Virgin and Child*, c.1315

Detail of Duccio's *Virgin and Child*

Tiepolo, *An Allegory with Venus and Time*, 1758

Gustave Courbet, *The Burial at Ornans*, 1849–50

A DORLING KINDERSLEY BOOK

For David

Project editor Phil Hunt
Art editor Mark Johnson Davies
Assistant editor Peter Jones
Design assistant Simon Murrell
Senior editor Gwen Edmonds
Managing editor Sean Moore
Managing art editor Toni Kay
US editor Laaren Brown
Picture researchers Julia Harris-Voss, Jo Evans
DTP designer Zirrinia Austin
Production controller Meryl Silbert

First published in Canada in 1994 by
Stoddart Publishing Co. Limited
34 Lesmill Road,.Toronto, Canada M3B2T6

This Eyewitness ®/™ Art book
first published in Great Britain in 1994 by
Dorling Kindersley Limited,
9 Henrietta Street, London WC2E 8PS

Canadian Cataloguing in Publication Data

Welton, Jude.
Looking at paintings

(Eyewitness art)
Includes index.
ISBN 0-7737-2768-X

1. Painting. 2. Art appreciation. I. Title.
II. Series: Eyewitness art (Don Mills, Ont.)
ND1143.W45 1994   750'.1'1   C93-095253-7

Colour reproduction by GRB Editrice s.r.l.
Printed in Italy by A. Mondadori Editore, Verona

Detail of Rubens's *The Château de Steen*

Peter Paul Rubens,
The Château de Steen, 1636

Contents

J. M.W. Turner,
Yacht Approaching the Coast, c.1835–40

A silent dialogue

When you look at a painting, you establish a silent dialogue with the picture before you. We bring our expectations, imagination, and taste to the experience, and the longer and closer we look, the more the painting reveals itself. Yet it is sometimes difficult to understand the visual language the artist has used: time and culture may distance us from the painting; it may depict an unfamiliar subject, or have no recognizable subject at all. Considering certain questions – about imagery, composition, color, and style, as well as about facts such as who the artist was, when it was painted, and why – can help us gain new insights. But a picture's particular appeal can never be fully explained: it remains and deepens with every viewing.

The Montefeltro Altarpiece

PIERO DELLA FRANCESCA

1472–74; 97¾ x 67 in (248 x 170 cm); oil on panel

This is one of the most closely scrutinized paintings in the history of art, and still one of the most mysterious. It shows the "donor" who commissioned the painting with the Madonna and Child, saints, and angels in a church. The figures stretch across the picture, their static poses, lowered eyes, and unconnected gazes creating a solemn stillness, accentuated by the composition's geometric balance.

QUESTIONS OF PAINTING

There are a number of questions we can ask when we see a painting, including:

Who painted it, when, and why? What is it "about"?
Why was that subject chosen and how was it interpreted?
In what style is it painted? Does it look realistic?
What kind of composition is it?
What colors are used? Are they bright? Subdued?
What kind of paint is it? What is it painted on?
Do I like it?

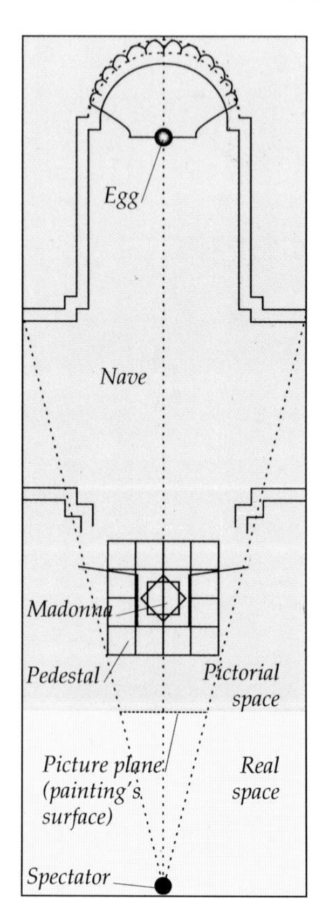

PICTORIAL SPACE

Many pictures aim to create the illusion that real, three-dimensional space exists beyond the picture's flat surface. Using perspective, artists can imitate the way objects appear smaller and parallel lines converge with increasing distance from the viewer. A "bird's-eye view" diagram of this painting's imaginary space – in relation to a spectator – is shown, left.

• Manipulating perspective, Piero has created an optical illlusion to shrink the church's long nave. This makes the figures appear huge.

• The picture plane acts like a "window" through which the spectator views the painting.

THE MYSTERY OF THE EGG
Paintings often contain symbols, and speculation about this painting has centered on the symbolic meaning of the egg. Its shape is echoed by the oval head of the Madonna below, who is encircled by figures as the egg is encircled by the shell. Such formal links may suggest a link in meaning: not only is an egg a symbol of birth and creation, personified by the infant Jesus, but this is an ostrich egg – traditionally linked with the miraculous Virgin birth. In this painting it may also refer to the "miraculous" birth of the donor's son (see below right).

The egg identifies the setting as a church, since ostrich eggs were hung above altars

Piero originally gave the Madonna a headdress like this, but another artist painted it out

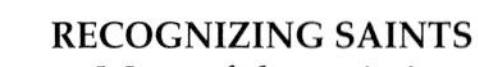

RECOGNIZING SAINTS
Most of the artist's contemporaries would have recognized the saints in the painting. St. Peter Martyr was usually shown in his friar's robes, displaying his fatal head wound (sometimes with a hatchet or sword embedded in his skull).

UNFINISHED SECTIONS
With mannered delicacy, St. Francis displays a jeweled crucifix and draws aside his robe to reveal one of his stigmata, the marks that correspond to Christ's wounds. Here, the thinly applied paint shows us that the picture is unfinished – which explains why the usual haloes have not yet been added to the holy figures.

COLOR AND DETAIL
Passing centuries create physical changes as well as cultural distance. This painting's silvery light was hidden until the work was cleaned in the 1980s, when what was thought to be a warm, golden glow was exposed as dirty varnish. This detail reveals the fineness of technique: the angel's body is shown through shimmering highlights and shaded folds of diaphanous gauze.

Light reflects off the crystal pendant

The baby may signify both Jesus and Federico's own son

BIRTH AND DEATH
When Renaissance artists showed the baby Jesus asleep across his mother's lap, they knew that contemporary viewers would be reminded of another then-familiar image, the *Pietà*, in which the Madonna is shown mourning over the body of her dead Son. This reference to birth and death is particularly relevant, since it seems that Federico commissioned this painting to commemorate the birth of his only son, and the death of his beloved wife.

BATTISTA SFORZA AND FEDERICO DA MONTEFELTRO
Piero della Francesca; c.1472–74; diptych (two panels framed together) 18½ x 13 in (47 x 33 cm) each; tempera on wood
In the *Montefeltro Altarpiece* Federico is in armor, offering protection to the Church. Here, he is in court dress with his late wife, parted by death but inseparable in art. Looking at the diptych alongside the altarpiece deepens our appreciation of both works. Though Battista is physically absent from the altarpiece, she is central to its existence. After eight daughters, she had vowed to give her life if she were blessed with a son: Guidobaldo was born in January 1472; she died of pneumonia in July.

Size, shape, and scale

THE PAINTINGS REPRODUCED on these pages appear to have approximately the same dimensions, yet their real sizes vary as much as their shapes: Gustave Courbet's *Burial at Ornans* is actually some 5,000 times greater in area than Nicholas Hilliard's miniature portrait, shown beneath it. When we look at a painting in a gallery, or in the setting for which it was originally intended, its physical size has an immediate effect on us. That effect, along with many others, is lost in photographic reproduction: nothing can replace the experience of seeing a work of art in the original. Like its size, the physical shape of a painting is perceived instantly. Shapes can vary enormously according to context, function, and taste. Even in the common, rectangular format, a painting's particular proportions may be chosen deliberately with regard to content and composition. Most individual portraits, for example, are vertical, and most landscape paintings are horizontal. Both these formats reflect the subjects' characteristics as well as emphasizing the way we perceive them in life: the verticality of the human figure as opposed to the horizontal-dominated landscape, which our eyes scan from side to side.

THE ANGEL GABRIEL
Giovanni del Ponte;
early 15th century; 16¾ x 9½ in (42.5 x 24 cm)
For centuries, the majority of European paintings had a religious purpose, which was expressed in their shape and size as well as in their Christian imagery. Many altarpieces, such as the one that originally included this panel, were impressively large, splendidly fashioned objects that reflected God's glory and the Church's power. They often had numerous painted panels set in an elaborate architectural framework. Here, the painting and its elegantly shaped frame form a perfectly integrated unit.

Original – but regilded – frame

Semicircular arches echo the tondo's shape

Architecture jutting into the painting leads the eye into the composition

TONDO: ADORATION OF THE KINGS
Sandro Botticelli; c.1470–75; 51¾ in (131.5 cm) diameter; egg tempera on poplar
The circular painting, or tondo, was popular among 15th-century Italian artists, who were attracted by the compositional challenges that the format offered. Botticelli has constructed a masterful composition, using converging lines to lead the eye to the center, and to the Virgin and Child. Though diminished in size because of perspective, their significance is emphasized by their position and by the architecture behind them, the lines of which add a sense of structure and stability to the design.

THE BURIAL AT ORNANS
Gustave Courbet; 1849–50; 124 x 263 in (315 x 668 cm)
Size and scale are significant indicators of a painting's status (pp. 28–29). This vast canvas, packed with more than 50 life-size figures, caused an outcry when it was first exhibited at the Paris Salon in 1850. It depicted an ordinary country scene on the monumental scale usually confined to grand history paintings – thereby elevating the working-class figures to heroic status. Shocked viewers considered it "a glorification of vulgarity" and branded Courbet a revolutionary socialist.

MORNING GLORY WITH BLACK
Georgia O'Keeffe; 1926; 36 x 30 in (91.5 x 76 cm)
Equally important to a picture's dimensions is the relative size of the painted object to the real object, and the extent to which the image fills the frame. Flower paintings, traditionally small and associated with femininity, were transformed by O'Keeffe through scale. She magnified the small blooms to fill her large canvases and obtain a powerful monumentality.

ALICE HILLIARD
Nicholas Hilliard; 1578; 2¼ in (6 cm) diameter, shown actual size; watercolor on vellum (backed with playing card)
Unlike Courbet's painting, which was designed for public display, this tiny portrait was intended for a more private, intimate gaze. While the huge size of the *Burial* lends it status, the very minuteness of this work, allied to its exquisitely refined technique, gives it a gemlike preciousness.

Composition

WHETHER CREATING a figurative work – one in which elements from the physical world are represented – or an abstract one, the artist has to divide up the picture surface and compose the elements of the image. On one level, this may be simply a matter of creating a pleasing design. But composition can have a powerful effect on the way the spectator responds to the picture. Symmetrical, balanced paintings can evoke a mood of tranquillity, stillness, and harmony, and – particularly in large-scale works – can create a sense of formal grandeur. Asymmetrical, deliberately unbalanced compositions may heighten the sense of drama or unease, or create the effect of dynamic action. Composition can also help tell the story, by leading the eye through the picture in a way that helps the spectator to "read" the narrative as the artist intended.

ST. GEORGE AND THE DRAGON
Tintoretto; c.1560 62 x 39½ in (152.5 x 100.5 cm)
While Giotto's Joachim moves toward the right, leading the eye on to the next panel in the narrative sequence, Tintoretto's maiden rushes toward the spectator. Though she glances back over her shoulder into the middle distance where St. George (symbolizing Christianity) is slaying the dragon (symbolizing paganism), her outstretched hand seems to burst through the picture surface into real space. The dynamic twisting of her body, and the whirling red drapery, are echoed throughout the composition, in a powerful series of zigzagging diagonals.

THE EXPULSION OF JOACHIM
Giotto; c.1303–06; 72 x 72 in (183 x 183 cm); fresco
In this intensely moving image, the first panel of the narrative cycle painted for the Arena Chapel (p. 31), composition helps to express the personal drama involved in the biblical story. Clutching his rejected sacrificial lamb to his chest, the aging Joachim is expelled from the temple because he is childless. As another man receives blessing, safely enclosed within the walls of the temple, Joachim is literally pushed off the edge into the void. The empty strip of blue space emphasizes his isolation.

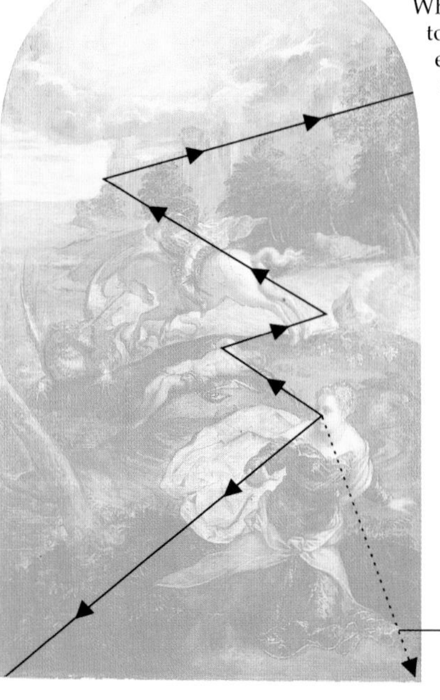

ZIGZAG DESIGN
Tintoretto's picture is composed of opposing diagonals that lead the eye to specific points in the drama: from the fleeing maiden, to the dragon's latest victim, to the lunging figure of St. George, and finally to a distant walled city, where – legend has it – these events took place.

Diagonal lines lead the eye both into the painting and out toward the spectator

THE EMBARKATION OF THE QUEEN OF SHEBA
Claude Lorrain (Claude Gellée); 1648; 58½ x 76¼ in (148.5 x 193.5 cm)
Artists may favor particular types of composition, repeating them in a number of paintings. Claude Lorrain often composed idealized landscapes and seascapes such as this one – with buildings (or trees) positioned on either side of the canvas, leading the eye down a visual tunnel toward a pale and luminous horizon. Such compositions inspired other painters, including Turner (p. 17).

THE DEATH OF MARAT
Jacques-Louis David; 1793; 65 x 50½ in (165 x 128.5 cm)
The tremendous impact of this large picture can only be fully felt when standing in front of it. It shows a martyr of the French Revolution, murdered in his bath by a young woman; her letter requesting an audience is in his bloodied hand. David has composed an image of remarkable simplicity and grandeur, stripping away irrelevant details – such as Marat's fashionably decorated bathroom. The top half is empty; all attention is concentrated on Marat. Marking the halfway point across the painting is the pen in Marat's hand, indicating how he worked tirelessly for the people. Outlined against the dark background, his pose is deliberately reminiscent of images of the dead Christ, while his vinegar-soaked turban – worn to alleviate a skin complaint – gives him the noble air of a classical hero.

HANEDA FERRY AND THE BENTEN SHRINE
Hiroshige; 1858; woodblock print
The art of the Japanese print reveals an approach to composition very different from that of Western artists. This print illustrates Japanese design at its most striking. The artist has adopted a startling viewpoint, as if sitting beside the ferryman: the river scene is framed by the uncomfortably close-up view of his hairy limbs. Areas of flat, unmodulated color combine with bold, stylized outlines to accentuate the surface pattern. By cropping off the figure of the ferryman at the picture's edges, the artist has used composition to create an impression of unposed spontaneity.

BLUE AND SILVER – SCREEN WITH OLD BATTERSEA BRIDGE
James McNeill Whistler; 1871–72; 76¾ x 71¾ in (195 x 182 cm); distemper and gold paint on brown paper laid on canvas
Whistler was one of many 19th-century Western artists influenced by the compositional devices used in Japanese prints. On this Japanese-style screen, the simple lines of the bridge are silhouetted against subtle washes of color that suggest the sky and river. As the bridge's gentle curve spans both panels of the screen, it emphasizes the surface pattern. The asymmetrical positioning of the bridge is typical of Japanese composition. It leaves the right-hand panel virtually empty apart from the wide, dark line cutting through the golden circle of the moon.

Using color

AN ARTIST'S CHOICE of colors is of fundamental importance. Color may be used descriptively – to re-create the actual colors seen by the artist's eye – but it does not have to be. Its possible roles in a painting are numerous. In addition to helping represent three-dimensional forms, it can be used decoratively, or to express emotion, or to create a mood. Sometimes, it may have symbolic significance. The Virgin Mary is traditionally shown wearing a blue cloak, for example, blue being the symbolic color of heaven (of which she is queen). Color is also one of the means by which the artist can create the illusion of space (pp. 16–17). The range and combination of colors used in a painting has a powerful effect on the character of the work: there may be a wide or narrow range; the colors may be harmonious or discordant, bright or subdued, closely linked or vividly contrasting.

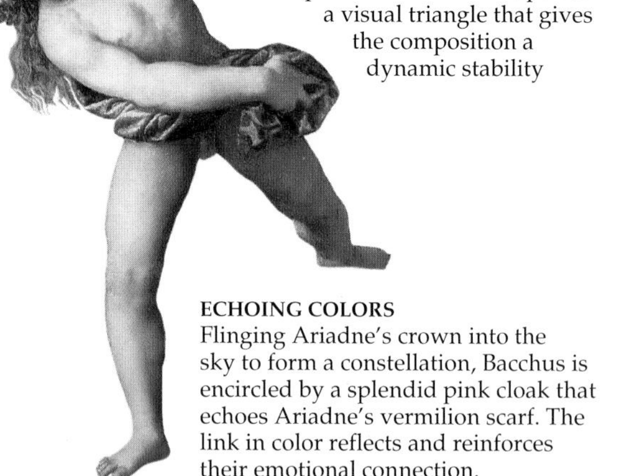

The outlines of billowing pink fabric form the apex of a visual triangle that gives the composition a dynamic stability

ECHOING COLORS
Flinging Ariadne's crown into the sky to form a constellation, Bacchus is encircled by a splendid pink cloak that echoes Ariadne's vermilion scarf. The link in color reflects and reinforces their emotional connection.

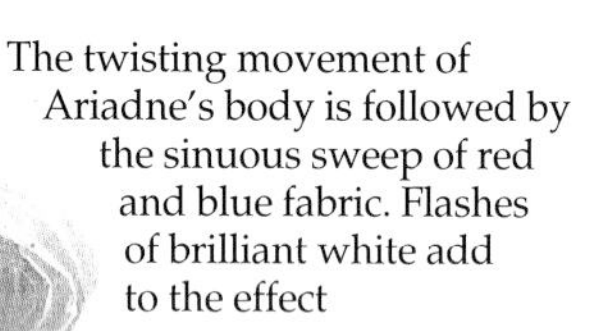

The twisting movement of Ariadne's body is followed by the sinuous sweep of red and blue fabric. Flashes of brilliant white add to the effect

BOLDNESS AND SUBTLETY
Titian exploits bold color contrasts, setting blue against brilliant red, but he also juxtaposes closer colors, such as the ultramarine of Ariadne's robe and the blue-green sea. Avoiding imbalance, he has used ultramarine again for the skirt of the cymbal player, whose pose also echoes that of Ariadne.

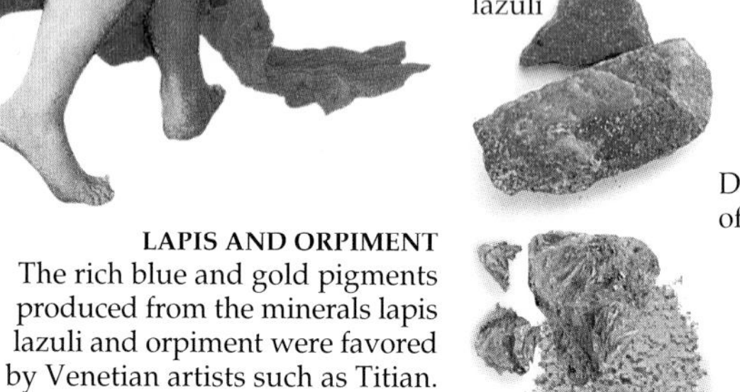

Lapis lazuli

Orpiment

Detail of sky

Golden urn

LAPIS AND ORPIMENT
The rich blue and gold pigments produced from the minerals lapis lazuli and orpiment were favored by Venetian artists such as Titian. Lapis lazuli was (and still is) a rare mineral: until the 19th century, it was only available from Afghanistan.

Bacchus and Ariadne

TITIAN *1520–23; 69 x 75 in (175 x 190.5 cm)*
This vibrant painting depicts the meeting of the wine god Bacchus with his wife-to-be Ariadne. Its most immediately striking aspect is the vast expanse of intense blue. Made from the mineral lapis lazuli, this ultramarine blue was rare, laborious to produce, and more expensive than gold. It is used here with conspicuous extravagance and dramatic effect. Bacchus and Ariadne gaze at each other across the heavenly blue, the red and pink of their robes set in brilliant contrast against it. Beneath the diagonal of their gaze, the dominant colors are reddish browns and greens.

YELLOW LANDSCAPE, PONT AVEN
Roderic O'Conor; 1892; 26½ x 36¼ in (67.5 x 92 cm)
Ribbons of color run in alternating stripes through the sun-drenched landscape in a sweeping, rhythmic pattern. O'Conor has used brilliant contrasts, which are particularly intense where "complementary" colors are placed next to one another. In painting, the main pairs of complementary colors are red/green, violet/yellow, and blue/orange. While these complementaries produce gray if mixed together, each appears more vivid if they are set beside each other.

YOUNG WOMAN HOLDING A BLACK CAT
Gwen John; c.1920–25; 18 x 11½ in (45.5 x 29.5 cm)
While artists such as O'Conor (above) and Bell (far right) used heightened color to achieve their effects, Gwen John created subtle and closely related rather than contrasting colors. Dressed in gray, the girl sits impassively with the black cat on her lap The quiet, restrained quality of the subject is perfectly complemented by this color scheme. There is a restricted range of colors, all with similar tonal values: the mauve of the seat is scarcely distinguishable from the gray-brown background.

MRS. ST. JOHN HUTCHINSON
Vanessa Bell; 1915; 29 x 22¾ in (73.5 x 58 cm); oil on board
One of the most significant developments in early 20th-century painting was that many artists ceased to use color simply to record what they observed in the "real" world. They became concerned with exploiting the effects of color for its own sake, rather than using it strictly as a realistic element in a painting. Here, the arrangement of bold colors on the picture surface is as important as the likeness of the portrait itself. Indeed, the figure becomes part of the arrangement, the bright pink flesh merging with the pink background. The blue "whites" of the eyes are particularly striking.

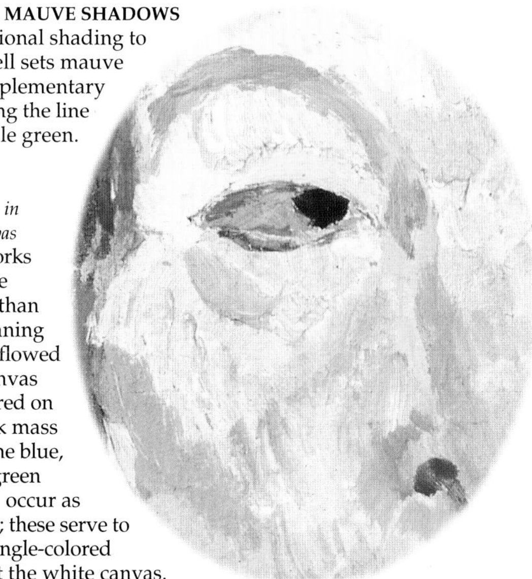

MAUVE SHADOWS
Instead of using traditional shading to model the features, Bell sets mauve shadows against complementary yellow highlights, marking the line of the cheekbone with pale green.

ALEPH
Morris Louis; 1960; 93 x 104 in (236 x 264 cm); acrylic on canvas
Morris Louis's abstract works explore the effects of pure color as it "stains" rather than "paints" the canvas. Thinning the acrylic paint so that it flowed easily across the huge canvas and soaked in, Louis poured on color after color. The dark mass has accumulated where the blue, yellow, orange, red, and green overlap. Subtle variations occur as two or more colors merge; these serve to accentuate the purity of single-colored prongs that are set against the white canvas.

Lines and colors

BY LOOKING closely at two apparently dissimilar paintings – one that consists of an arrangement of lines and color with no recognizable "subject," the other with a detailed story to tell – we can see how the same basic artistic means, color and composition, are at work in both. Though the planned organization of the picture surface is more immediately obvious in Mondrian's *Composition with Red, Yellow, and Blue* than in Poussin's *Adoration of the Golden Calf* – painted three hundred years previously – a rigorous, deliberate quality of order and balance unites them. Color and composition are interconnected in any painting: in Titian's *Bacchus and Ariadne* (p. 12), for example, the "empty" but intense area of blue in the top left is counterbalanced by the busily detailed but less intensely colored bottom right. On these pages, both artists have constructed their images according to a geometric framework and distributed their colors throughout the picture surface to create a sense of equilibrium and harmony.

Charcoal

Ruler

MEASURING UP
For centuries, artists have used tools to draw in the main lines of their compositions before applying paint. Mondrian used charcoal and a ruler. The crossing of horizontal and vertical lines at right angles was central to his artistic purpose – for him this was the "principal opposition" that expressed "abiding equilibrium."

CHESSBOARD GRID
Though the metaphysical ideas that lay behind his work were complex, Mondrian's means of expressing them appear deceptively simple. The system used here is based on eight squares, like a chessboard.

PRECISE ARRANGEMENT
Placed over an eight-by-eight grid, the balanced irregularity of the latticework becomes clear. Lines vary in width as well as spacing. Mondrian adjusted the relationships between line and color with meticulous care. Only the large square of red is bounded on all four sides by black.

Composition with Red, Yellow, and Blue

PIET MONDRIAN *c.1937–42; 27 x 28 in (69 x 72 cm)*
The title of this painting is significant – it is "about" composition and color. Mondrian developed a new artistic language, reducing natural forms to their abstract essence. In this picture, he has rejected any reference to the "real" world. Limiting his vocabulary to the most basic elements – straight lines, primary colors (blue, red, and yellow), and black and white – he sought to create pure painting that expressed universal truths.

The Adoration of the Golden Calf

NICOLAS POUSSIN *c.1636–37; 60¾ x 84½ in (154.5 x 214.5 cm)*

This biblical scene depicts the moment when Moses, coming down from Mount Sinai (where he has received the Ten Commandments written on the Tablets of Law), discovers the Israelites worshiping an idol – a Golden Calf made by his brother Aaron. Poussin has structured the composition in such a way that every element is designed to present the narrative with clarity and underline the moral seriousness of the subject. Key figures or groups in the drama are given their own clearly defined areas within the basic geometric framework (right); gestures are precise and eloquent, and color is deliberately restrained and balanced.

GEOMETRIC CLARITY
The underlying geometry of the composition is clear. A horizontal line running across the altar and between Aaron's uplifted hands intersects with a vertical that runs up the side of the altar, dividing the canvas – and the narrative – into four main sections. The top left contains Moses, Joshua, two frightened figures, and the Calf. The idol is in the same main quadrant as Moses, but is isolated in its own invisible rectangle. In the section below, idolatrous revelers dance in angular motion, unaware of Moses's approach. In the bottom right, figures reach in adoration toward the Calf, one group forming a triangle that reinforces one of the picture's main diagonals. Behind them, the figures' horrified gestures indicate that they have seen their wrathful leader.

BALANCE AND UNITY
Poussin has limited his range of colors and distributed the main ones – blue, red, and orange – throughout the painting to enhance the painting's balance as well as its unity. The foreground figures form two distinct groups, differentiated by their poses, but clearly linked by virtue of the color combinations.

Light, shade, and space

IN PAINTING, as in the real world we learn about objects' shapes and surfaces by the fall of light and shadow. Many paintings create the illusion that solid objects exist in three-dimensional space beyond their flat surface. To imitate the way we perceive real space, artists use conventions of linear and aerial perspective (pp. 6 & 18–19). The first re-creates the optical illusion that objects grow smaller and parallel lines converge as the distance from the viewer increases. The second mimics the atmospheric effect that makes distant objects appear pale and blue. One great challenge for a painter is to show space stretching from foreground to background. It is easier to achieve with interiors and urban scenes than with landscapes, as there are straight lines that can be exploited.

A VISUAL LEAP
A ridge (or terrace, as in Leonardo's *Mona Lisa*, p. 60) was a useful device for making the transition from foreground to background, without the need of a gradual recession through the middle distance. But here it is used to separate two incompatible viewpoints. The foreground figures are painted as if seen from below – appropriately, since the painting would have been placed high up behind an altar. From this position, the landscape beyond would be hidden by the ridge.

THE MARTYRDOM OF ST. SEBASTIAN
Antonio & Piero del Pollaiuolo; 1475; 114¾ x 79¾ in (291.5 x 202.5 cm); oil on poplar
The space in this altarpiece is obviously inconsistent, yet the image is so powerful that the viewer can suspend disbelief. The spectator looks up the ridge at the figures, who are forcefully modeled in light and shade – and down onto the distant vista. In reality, it would be impossible to see these foreground and background views simultaneously.

HUNTERS IN THE SNOW
Pieter Bruegel the Elder; 1565; 46 x 63¾ in (117 x 162 cm)
In this remarkable painting of peasants trudging through a cold winter landscape, the eye is led across and into the picture by the movement of the hunters and their dogs, and by the diagonal of dark trees. Silhouetted against the white snow, the receding trunks mark a rhythmic progression into space toward tiny distant figures and a mountainous panorama.

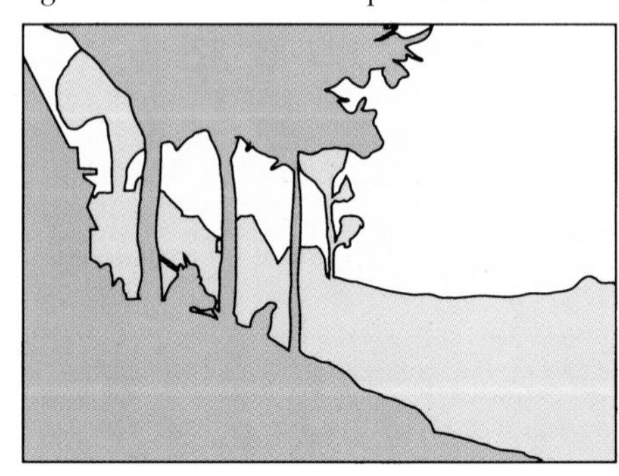

LAYERED SPACE
The picture space does not flow continuously, but exists almost as flat pieces of stage scenery, each one punctuating the next step in the spatial sequence.

THE CHATEAU DE STEEN
Peter Paul Rubens; c.1636; 52 x 90½ in (132 x 223 cm)
This huge autumnal landscape is a celebration of the country estate that the artist had recently bought. It combines a mass of minutely observed detail with a vast panoramic view. Space stretches to the distant, flat horizon, where the town of Antwerp shimmers in a blue haze. As a laden cart sets off to market, the entire scene is bathed in the golden light of an autumn morning.

WARM AND COOL COLORS
This detail shows Rubens's use of the effects of warm and cool colors in the creation of the picture's space. So-called warm colors – those at the red end of the spectrum – appear to come toward the viewer. Cool colors – those toward the blue end – appear to recede. The red berries and orange-gold hues of bark and autumn foliage in the foreground appear to advance, while progressively bluer greens lead the eye back to the blue horizon.

A BOY BRINGING POMEGRANATES
Pieter de Hoogh; 1662; 29 x 23¾ in (73.5 x 60 cm)
Compared to landscapes, interior scenes give artists more opportunites for articulating space. Here, De Hoogh makes use of the lines of architectural elements to create a sense of spatial recession. Converging lines of receding floor tiles measure the movement into depth and lead the eye back to the small figure at the far doorway. From the shady foreground entrance, an alternating pattern of light-dark-light marks successive courtyards. The exquisitely warm light models forms, defines space, and reinforces the tranquil mood.

YACHT APPROACHING THE COAST
J.M.W. Turner; c.1835–40; 40¼ x 56 in (102 x 142 cm)
The subject here seems to be light itself. Though this brilliant study may appear formless, it is structured according to the compositional principles that Turner so admired in Claude Lorrain (p.11), leading the eye back toward a molten white horizon.

Illusion and reality

TRICKING THE EYE
In this detail from a Renaissance altarpiece (p. 38), the artist uses the type of illusionism known as *trompe l'oeil* (French: "deceives the eye"). The fruit is made to appear as though it is actually tied and nailed onto the architectural plinth of the altarpiece.

FOR CENTURIES, most artists aimed to make their painted objects appear like real objects occupying real space. And many people still judge a painting according to how "real" it looks. But in the 20th century, there has been a fundamental shift away from the notion that a painting exists to represent an illusion of observable reality. The Cubists first broke with the conventions of illusionism. Rather than showing objects from a single, fixed viewpoint (as in a still photograph), which is necessary for the creation of a visual illusion, they used multiple viewpoints – fragmenting objects by depicting them from a number of angles. Since then, non-representational, abstract art has developed, and many artists have rejected the idea that a painting needs to "look like" anything apart from itself – it has its own reality.

PERSPECTIVE LINES
In accordance with the laws of perspective, lines lead into pictorial space and converge at a "vanishing point." Here, they cross near the woman's heart, perhaps to reinforce the painting's theme of love.

COMPUTER RECONSTRUCTION
The illusory space in Vermeer's painting is so precise that experts at the Open University in Milton Keynes, England were able to create a computer model. On screen, the scene can be viewed from all angles – including this aerial view.

A Young Woman Standing at a Virginal

JAN VERMEER *c.1670; 20¼ x 17¾ in (51.5 x 45 cm)*
Vermeer probably constructed this painting using a camera obscura – a viewing box with lens and mirrors through which an image of the scene could be projected onto a screen, then traced by the artist. Various peculiarities point to its use, such as the looming chair in the foreground and out-of-focus areas around the highlights. The painting may have a hidden theme of faithful love – symbolized by the picture of Cupid with a single playing card.

CLARINET AND BOTTLE OF RUM ON A MANTELPIECE
Georges Braque; 1913; 32 x 23½ in (81 x 60 cm)
In this Cubist still life, Braque uses multiple viewpoints, breaking up objects into geometric facets. Recognizable fragments and words allude to the objects and the musical theme.

EUCLIDIAN WALKS
René Magritte; 1955; 64 x 51¼ in (162.5 x 130 cm)
The flat surface of a painting has often been likened to a window through which reality can be viewed. Here, Magritte wittily comments on the relationship between reality and its painted equivalent. He places a canvas in front of a window so that the "painted" view extends beyond the canvas edge. But the view through the window is not "real" either: it too is painted. The similarity between the receding street and the conical tower highlights the ambiguities of pictorial representation.

COSSACKS
Wassily Kandinsky; 1910–11; 37¼ x 51¼ in (94.5 x 130 cm)
This canvas contains references to the visible world: to the left, two horses rear up, their red-hatted Cossack riders swinging mauve sabers; to the right are more Cossacks, and guns. But the painting does not try to look "real" – it uses the abstract effects of color and line to embody the idea of conflict. Kandinsky later developed a purely abstract art to express invisible, spiritual reality.

Paintings in context

WE OFTEN LOOK at paintings out of their original context. But to fully appreciate the particular character of a work of art, we need to consider its original function and setting, and think how those affected its form and content. Most paintings were not made to be hung beside others in a gallery; they were commissioned or sold for a set purpose. That purpose might have been anything from aiding private religious devotions (right) to decorating the ceiling of an aristocrat's palace (second right). The imagery, style, size, and viewpoint of a painting depend largely on why it was painted, for whom it was painted, and where it was intended to be seen.

THE MOCKING OF CHRIST
Fra Angelico (Guido di Pietro); 1440–41; 76¾ x 62½ in (195 x 159 cm)
This painting dominates the wall of Cell 7 in the Florentine priory of San Marco. The quality of restraint is characteristic of Fra Angelico's work, but the treatment of the subject reflects the painting's purpose. All sense of real violence is omitted from a scene in which Christ is blindfolded, beaten, and spat upon. The image was composed to aid the friars' meditation – disembodied emblems of Christ's suffering were more suitable than an unsettlingly realistic narrative.

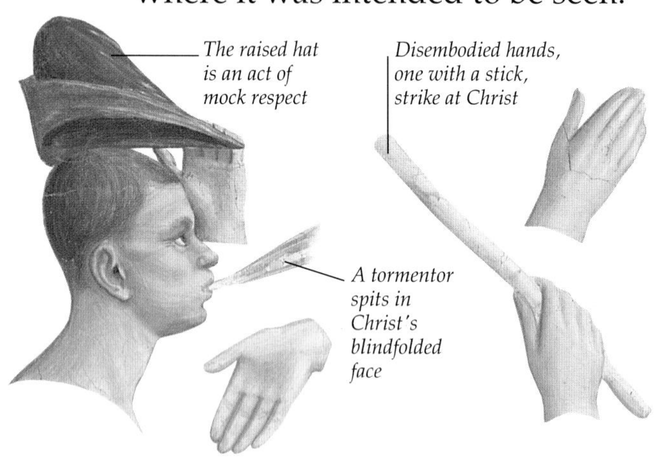

COMBINED EMBLEMS
The details of the indignities suffered by Christ are combined from two separate scenes – the mocking of Christ and the crowning with thorns before the crucifixion.

THE PRIORY OF SAN MARCO
All the cells and corridors of San Marco are adorned with scenes from the life of Christ.

THE LAST SUPPER
Leonardo da Vinci; c.1495–97; 166 x 355 in (421.5 x 901.5 cm)
Leonardo's *Last Supper* was, like Angelico's painting, painted for a priory. Filling the end wall of the refectory at Santa Maria delle Grazie in Milan, it depicts the moment when Christ tells his followers that one of them would betray him; their shocked reactions contrast with His calm. This was an understandably popular subject for such a setting: it appeared as if Christ and the Apostles were eating with the friars.

AN ALLEGORY WITH VENUS AND TIME
Giovanni Battista Tiepolo; c.1758; 115 x 74¾ in (292 x 190 cm)
Framed in its curved border, Tiepolo's painting was part of a ceiling decoration in a Venetian palace. Despite its decorative beauty, it was not merely ornamental: the subject was chosen to celebrate the birth of an heir in the family that commissioned it. Venus has given birth to the Trojan hero Aeneas, the baby cradled by Time, whose dropped scythe indicates immortality. The figures are painted as if seen from below – both because they are up in the clouds, and because the painting was set in the ceiling.

DECORATED FLORENTINE WEDDING CHEST
Zanobi di Domenico (carving); Jacopo del Sellaio and Biagio d'Antonio (painting); 1472; 83½ x 76 x 30 in (212 x 193 x 76 cm)
Some of the paintings that we might now see hanging on a wall originally came from pieces of furniture. Their original setting would have determined not only their shape and size, but also their subject matter. A long painted panel from the Italian Renaissance, for example, may have been part of a *cassone* (betrothal chest) commissioned by a prosperous man at the time of his marriage. This is one of a rare pair of *cassoni*, each complete with its own back panel, or *spalliera*. It is adorned with suitably heroic tales from classical literature. In Florence, such items of painted furniture were usually destined for the *camera*, the principal living/sleeping room.

A NEW POSITION
Cima's altarpiece (far right) had been badly damaged over the centuries (p. 27) and was stored away from public view until restored to its present state. When the National Gallery's Sainsbury Wing opened in 1991, it was hung at the end of a long vista of receding columns in the new wing. Although its position does not re-create the effect of the original church setting, it illustrates how much our view of a painting is affected by the way it is hung. Here, position indicates significance, and the architectural setting emphasizes the painting's accurate use of perspective – most obvious in the receding tiles and coffering. Seen from a distance, and on approaching, the picture seems to continue the tunnel of space created by the avenue of columns.

THE INCREDULITY OF ST. THOMAS
Cima da Conegliano; 1504; 115¾ x 78½ in (294 x 199.5 cm)
This huge altarpiece was commissioned by a Venetian confraternity (a group of laypeople joined in shared devotions and good works). It depicts the group's patron saint Thomas, the apostle who doubted the Resurrection, examining the wounds Christ suffered when crucified.

Fresco, tempera, and oil

THE MATERIALS with which a painting is produced have a huge impact upon the way it looks. Major developments in style and technique have been closely linked to changes in the types of paints available. Until the development of oil paints in the 15th century, artists worked in fresco or tempera (see below), which have their own particular qualities of beauty, but which could not achieve the level of realism or variety of brushwork that was possible with oil. The fact that oil paint takes a long time to dry also allowed artists to make changes as they worked, which was difficult in fresco and tempera. Oil paints reigned supreme as the favored medium for 500 years, until the 1950s, when acrylics became a popular substitute (pp. 13, 21, & 47).

VIRGIN AND CHILD
Duccio de Buoninsegna; c.1315;
24⅛ x 15⅜ in (62 x 38 cm); egg tempera on wood
This tender image was the product of a long process. First, the wood was prepared with a smooth white layer of gesso (powdered gypsum mixed with glue). The main lines were drawn, then incised with a metal point. A red clay (bole) was brushed on the background before gold leaf was applied. Only then were the flesh and drapery painted with tempera.

FRESCO TECHNIQUE
Fresco is a method of wall painting in which the artist paints onto a coating of plaster. The bold simplicity that characterizes Giotto's work (p. 10) is partly due to the demands of the *buon fresco* (true fresco) technique. The design was drawn, then the paint applied to wet plaster; as it dried, pigment became permanently bound with plaster. Only as much fresh plaster as could be painted over in a day was applied at one time – the numbered sections indicate Giotto's daily progress.

Raw mineral azurite

Ground azurite

Egg yolk

GRINDING PAINTS
Pigments used in tempera painting were made from natural sources that included minerals, clays, wood, and plants. They were usually bought from an apothecary. Initially ground with a pestle and mortar, they were then ground with water on a stone slab to disperse the pigment.

TEMPERA AND GOLD
Tempera is more properly known as "egg tempera." Powdered pigments were mixed with egg yolk – the binding medium – to make a paint, which was applied in small, hatched strokes that dried almost immediately. For the background, gold leaf was burnished, and lines were incised with a compass, punches, and freehand drawing. Viewed by candlelight, the edges of indented lines caught the light and created a golden aura around the holy figures.

EYE CONTACT
This eye, painted by Antonello (right), turns to look at the spectator. Subtly graded and blended glazes define the curve and color of the skin, while the eye itself retains an uncannily real, translucent moistness.

PORTRAIT OF A MAN
Antonello da Messina; c.1475; 14 x 10 in (35.5 x 25.5 cm); oil on poplar
This stunning portrait illustrates the tremendous new possibilities offered by oil painting. The man's face leaps out at the viewer with a hyper-realism that is almost too intense, like a photograph in perfect focus. By using oil rather than egg as the medium, the artist could add the paint in fine, transparent glazes, each one subtly modifying the others. The light-reflecting properties of oil paint meant that it could depict natural surfaces such as skin in a much more realistic way than tempera. Early users, such as Antonello, concentrated on creating hitherto unknown levels of illusionism (p. 18).

Ultramarine

Spanish brown

Burnt sienna

Walnut oil

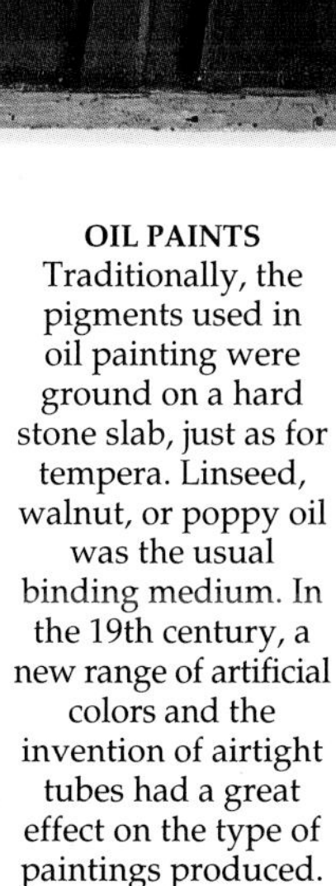

OIL PAINTS
Traditionally, the pigments used in oil painting were ground on a hard stone slab, just as for tempera. Linseed, walnut, or poppy oil was the usual binding medium. In the 19th century, a new range of artificial colors and the invention of airtight tubes had a great effect on the type of paintings produced.

Early tubes of oil paints

THE MORNING WALK
Thomas Gainsborough; 1785–86; 93 x 70½ in (236 x 179 cm)
In addition to enabling artists to create realistic images, oil paints also offered the possibility of using brushwork in an individual and expressive way. Unlike fresco and tempera, oils allowed a huge variety of "touch." Part of the appeal of paintings by Gainsborough is the sheer beauty of his brushwork. In this marriage portrait, the refinement of the scene is matched by the elegant subtlety of the artist's distinctive, feathery brushstrokes.

GAUZE AND SILK
Its transparency echoed in paint, Mrs. Hallett's gauze shawl floats across her arm, over her silk dress.

WOMAN AND CHILD IN THE GARDEN AT BOUGIVAL
Berthe Morisot; 1882; 24 x 28¾ in (59.6 x 73 cm); oil on unprimed canvas
Like her fellow Impressionists, Morisot rejected the tightly finished style of oil painting that dominated in the 19th century. Rather than hiding the painting process by blending brushstrokes until they were undetectable, she used her paint with astonishing freedom, slashing the strokes across the canvas.

Watercolor and pastel

WORKING ON PAPER in watercolor and pastel has traditionally been held to be less "significant" than painting in oil. Yet both media have long been popular, partly because of their qualities of immediacy and freedom. The portability of watercolor and the rapidity with which it dries makes it a natural medium for painting outdoors and for making on-the-spot studies. But watercolor is extremely versatile; it can be used to produce anything from tiny colored drawings to works with the detail and complexity of oils. Like watercolors, pastels are made from pigments bound with gum, but are produced as a stick of color. Since works in these media are often on a small scale and displayed in subdued lighting to prevent fading, the experience of looking at watercolors and pastels can be a more intimate one than looking at other kinds of painting.

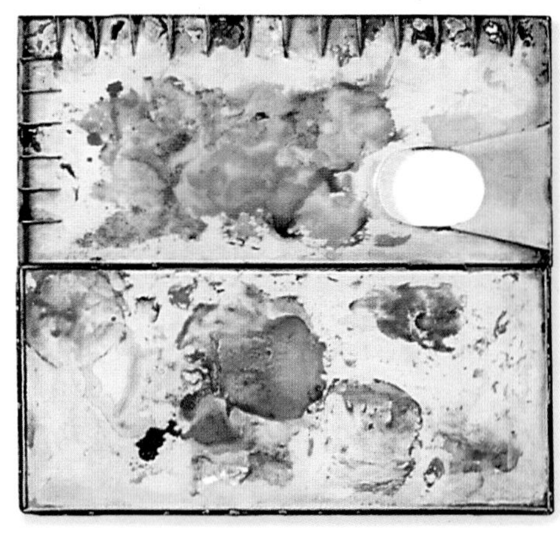

WATERCOLOR PALETTE
In watercolor palettes, such as James McNeill Whistler's (above), the blocks of pigments are bound with gum arabic, which is water-soluble. Transparent washes of color can be produced, through which the pale ground – most commonly paper – shows. A closely related medium is gouache, or bodycolor: water-soluble pigments are mixed with lead white to create an opaque (nontransparent) paint.

THOMAS BOLEYN
Hans Holbein; c.1535; 16 x 11½ in (40.5 x 29.5 cm); watercolor, chalk, and crayon on paper
For Hans Holbein, the German artist who achieved fame at the court of King Henry VIII, brilliant draftsmanship was central. He considered drawings such as this portrait of Thomas Boleyn to be valuable works in their own right, not just preliminary studies for oil portraits. This magnificent picture shows the wide range of media and techniques he exploited when working on paper. To obtain the likeness, he may have used a mechanical aid, tracing the outlines on glass with an oil crayon before transferring them to paper. Using colored chalks, India ink, and watercolor washes, he has combined boldness of technique and color with detail so fine that the individual hairs of Boleyn's ruddy beard can be distinguished. He makes powerful use of the pale ground, not just in the rapidly worked area of the clothes, but in the precisely drawn and delicately modeled face.

LAKE LUCERNE: SUNSET (SAMPLE STUDY)
J.M.W. Turner; 1844; 9½ x 12 in (24.5 x 30.5 cm); pencil and watercolor on paper
The transparency of watercolor makes it ideal for the painting of the most intangible elements of nature, light, and air. Turner used both oil (p. 17) and watercolor to capture the effects of the atmosphere. Here, he exploits the effect of overlapping exquisitely subtle washes of color. This is one of a number of "samples" from which prospective patrons could select a subject to be worked up as a finished painting.

THE PIPE BEARER
J. F. Lewis; 1859; 22 x 16 in (56 x 40.5 cm); pencil, watercolor, bodycolor on paper
This Victorian painting shows the watercolor medium used with a minuteness of touch and a density of color more often associated with oils. It was intended for exhibition, to be treated with the same seriousness as an oil painting. In its exotic subject matter, brilliant colors, and tiny, tightly controlled brushstrokes, it is typical of the images that Lewis labored over for 30 years. The same effects could be achieved in much less time and effort in oil, and he eventually had to abandon watercolor to provide himself with a greater income as an oil painter.

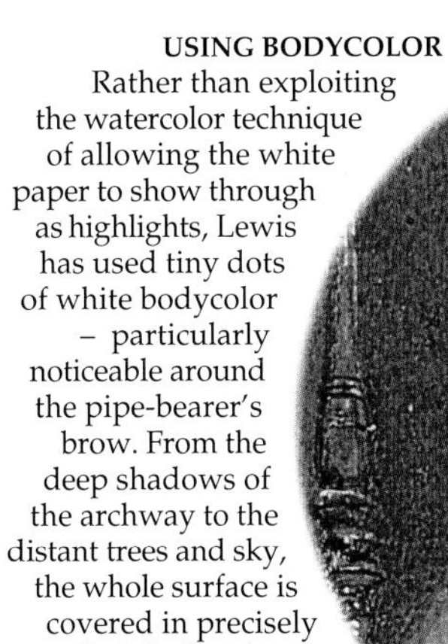

USING BODYCOLOR
Rather than exploiting the watercolor technique of allowing the white paper to show through as highlights, Lewis has used tiny dots of white bodycolor – particularly noticeable around the pipe-bearer's brow. From the deep shadows of the archway to the distant trees and sky, the whole surface is covered in precisely applied flecks of paint.

EXPERIMENTAL STYLE
Degas has captured the curve of the woman's bent wrists with apparently nonchalant ease, using his pastel in broad, hatched (parallel) lines and smudges to define forms and contour. With a limited range of colors, dominated here by the coppery tones of hair and sponge, he creates a vivid and varied surface texture.

A SUMMER PALACE AT THE FOOT OF A PRECIPITOUS MOUNTAIN
Artist unknown; Ming period (1368– 1644); 10 x 9 in (26 x 23 cm)
Watercolor has a much longer history in the East than in Europe. It was the Chinese who invented paper (in the first century), and they perfected the techniques of working on paper – and silk – with watercolors and ink. In this Chinese landscape, observed natural details combine with a strong sense of pictorial design. The delicately drawn trees, figures, and buildings of the palace are set against the broad washes and dramatic contours that define the form and texture of the mountains.

THE TUB
Edgar Degas; 1886; 23½ x 32½ in (60 x 83 cm); pastel on paper
Composition, viewpoint, and technique combine to make spectators feel they are looking through a keyhole, while the bather continues unaware. The deliberate asymmetry of the composition creates an "accidental" quality, while the high viewpoint – the spectator looks down on the bather – emphasizes the sense of voyeurism. Degas's bold use of pastel adds to the effect of unposed immediacy that he has contrived.

The picture surface

WHEN PAINTINGS are shown in reproduction, not only are they usually much reduced in size, but their surface detail is almost inevitably lost. One of the pleasures of looking at a painting directly is being able to study it closely – to peer at its brushwork, to see the weave of the canvas still evident where the paint is applied thinly, or to examine the thick, *impasto* paint that characterizes some artists' work. Close-up photographs such as the ones reproduced on these pages give a rare opportunity to appreciate the surface qualities of some of the paintings in this book, but there is still no substitute for looking at paintings in the original. Bear in mind, however, that with old paintings, the surface you are looking at may have changed significantly over the centuries, and may have been retouched by later hands.

ENAMEL FINISH
The gleaming, reflective surface of a shiny metal bucket, and its difference from the texture of the fabric beneath it, is captured with extraordinary minuteness in Dou's *Poulterer's Shop* (p. 29). The artist's slow, meticulous method is legendary and earned him an international reputation for the enamel-like finish of his paintings. He not only ground his own colors and made his own brushes, but was said not to start work until the dust had settled in his studio. The effect of his painstaking technique can be seen in this enlarged detail. It shows the painting's smooth, seamless texture, in which brushstrokes are imperceptible.

BRAVURA BRUSHWORK
The dashing, energetic brushwork on the sleeve of Hals's *Laughing Cavalier* (p. 45) is an outstanding example of the Dutch master's brilliant technique. Looking closely, we can see how Hals has used two main types of brushstrokes. In some areas, such as the band of orange-gold at the cuff, he has used broad, free strokes. But to pick out the intricate embroidery, he has used a small brush in bold but precise strokes that stand out against the sheen of the black sleeve.

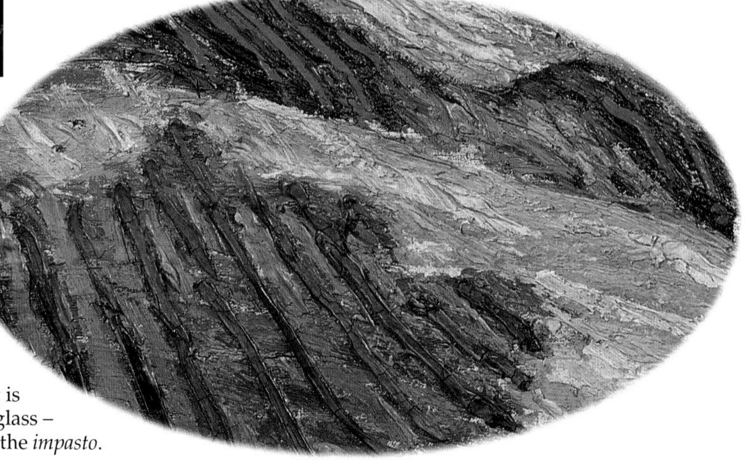

THICK IMPASTO
In complete contrast to Dou's glassy-smooth finish, Roderic O'Connor's *Yellow Landscape* (p. 13) is painted in heavy *impasto*. While the dryish paint retains the impression of individual brushstrokes, it forms a thick crust of vibrant color that covers the entire picture surface. Since it was painted in 1892, the surface has flattened in places, and the painting is now viewed beneath protective glass – slightly lessening the effect of the *impasto*.

SOAKING IN
There are no brushmarks to be seen in this detail from *Aleph* (p. 13). Morris Louis poured his thinned acrylic paint onto the canvas, which he had left unprimed so that the paint would soak in and stain, rather than sit on its surface. "Capillary scars" can be seen around the edges of the prongs of color, where paint and resin have separated. The regular texture of the canvas can also be detected.

The changing surface

A painting we see today may look very different from the way it appeared when it was first painted. The paint surface may have deteriorated or been damaged in numerous ways: colors fade, varnish darkens, canvases may be torn, the wooden panels on which a painting was made may warp or crack. Some changes need not be amended, but badly damaged – and badly retouched – paintings need to be restored if they are still to be enjoyed.

BEFORE RETOUCHING
This detail shows the sort of the damage that the team at the National Gallery, London, had to deal with when they restored Cima's *Incredulity of St. Thomas* (p. 21). The entire paint surface of this exceptionally damaged picture had blistered and flaked, large areas of paint had been lost completely. Needle holes, where past restorers had injected adhesives to treat the blisters, covered the surface. Earlier attempts at retouching can be seen in the darkened area of the mouth. The modern restorer's task was to clean and stabilize the painting making it legible again.

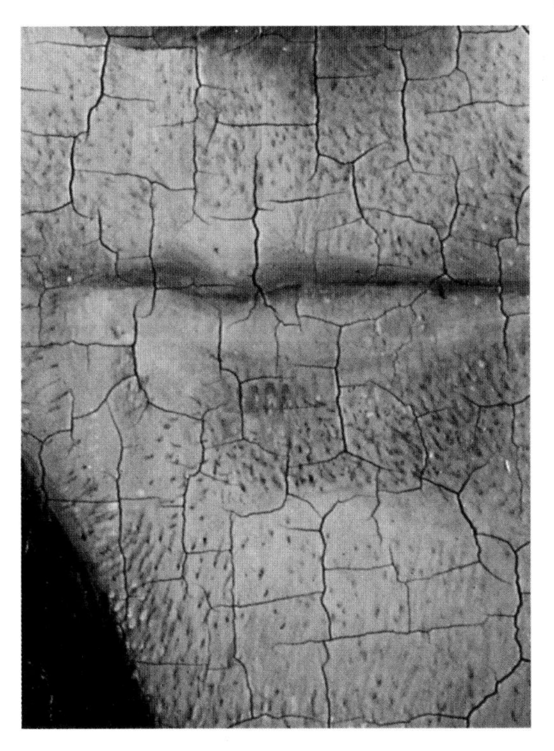

CRAQUELURE
The pattern of cracks, or craquelure, that covers van Eyck's *Man in a Turban* (p. 54) is due to the natural drying and aging of the paint. Though they are clearly visible in this magnified detail, the cracks are not immediately obvious when looking at the actual painting. Such craquelure does not detract from the painting's overall effect, and is not generally retouched.

APOSTLE RESTORED
This is what the apostle looked like after the restoration process. Technical analysis of the paint layers allowed restorers to determine Cima's technique and his exact choice of pigments: modern equivalents of his particular pigments were used in the retouching.

Subject matter and status

SINCE THE RENAISSANCE, certain categories, or genres, of painting have been considered more important than others. At the top of the hierarchy is "history painting" – serious, large-scale works representing scenes from history, the Bible, mythology, or literature. These have the public function of instructing and improving the spectator. Second comes portraiture, which may have a more private role than history painting, but which can depict important figures from the past and present. In third place are "genre" scenes, a somewhat confusing term in this context, used to describe small-scale scenes of everyday life. Rather than depicting inspirational heroes, they show people like ourselves – or worse. These first three categories all focus on human beings and their actions. The last two categories – landscape and still life – do not, which explains their low status, despite their popularity. Today, this pictorial hierarchy is not as entrenched as it was up until the 19th century, but it still has an influence on the kinds of paintings artists produce and the way we look at and respond to them.

ACADEMIC ART
Like all the heads of European art Academies from the 17th to the 19th century, Sir Joshua Reynolds (above), head of London's Royal Academy, upheld the primacy of "history painting."

THE OATH OF THE HORATII
Jacques-Louis David; 1784; 130¼ x 168½ in (331 x 428 cm)
In this supreme example of 18th-century history painting, David uses a classical subject (from ancient Rome) and style to celebrate and inspire patriotic duty. Profiled against the austere rhythm of a classical colonnade, the three Horatii brothers from Rome swear to fight three Curatii from Alba, sacrificing their life if necessary to prevent a war between the two cities. The message is uncompromising, and particularly relevant in pre-Revolutionary France: it is noble and virtuous to sacrifice individual happiness for the public cause.

GUERNICA
Pablo Picasso; 1937; 137½ x 305¾ in (349.5 x 776.5 cm)
Even larger and more somber than David's *Oath*, this is one of the great history paintings of our century. It was painted in response to the bombing of the northern Spanish town of Guernica by General Franco's right-wing forces during the Spanish Civil War (1936–39). Picasso makes no specific references to the actual event. But the jagged confusion of the composition and the unforgettable images of suffering, such as the screaming women and the terrified horse – according to Picasso a symbol of the people – vividly express the horror and inhumanity of war.

A POULTERER'S SHOP
Gerard Dou; c.1670; 22¾ x 26¾ in (58 x 68 cm); oil on wood
Its lowly subject-matter, small scale, and domestic setting distinguish this genre scene from the grandeur and moral seriousness of history painting. Framed within the arched window of the shop, two women admire a dead hare, while numerous dead birds in varying states of preparation are displayed in meticulous, if gruesome, detail on the ledge. In the ornate frieze below, chubby classical *putti* play with an unwilling goat, as a nearby caged cockerel is being fattened up – blissfully unaware of the fate that lies in store.

PORTRAIT OF A LADY IN YELLOW
Alesso Baldovinetti; c.1465; 24¾ x 16 in (63 x 40.5 cm); oil on wood
Pictured in profile against a plain blue background, this young noblewoman has not been identified, though the floral device on her sleeve probably relates to her family's coat of arms. Such profile portraits were popular in mid-15th century Italy, echoing the heads on antique coins.

HOARFROST
Camille Pissarro; 1873; 25½ x 36½ in (65 x 93 cm)
Boycotting the official Paris Salon, Pissarro showed this painting at the Impressionist exhibition in 1874. Upholding the academic values of the genres system, the Salon jury would have rejected such an unidealized landscape.

THE BRIOCHE
Jean-Baptiste-Siméon Chardin; 1763; 18½ x 22 in (47 x 56 cm)
Chardin's quiet, unpretentious still lifes brought him great acclaim in 18th-century France, and he is still acknowledged as one of the masters of the genre. Setting his objects against a plain, dark background, he creates a harmoniously balanced composition and gives individual textures an almost tangible reality.

Telling a story

NARRATIVE PICTURES, those that tell stories, were traditionally held to belong to the most worthy branch of painting – as long as the story being told had some religious, historical, or mythological significance. Visual storytelling can have many functions – to commemorate an event, educate those unable to read, illustrate a sermon, or make a moral point. It might seem that painting is less suited to storytelling than to other subject matter, since stories by their nature happen in sequence and a painting presents a single image. Yet paintings can unfold their narrative content in many ways: they can focus on one significant moment, or deliberately obscure the central point; some show a number of events simultaneously, while others present individual episodes in a kind of comic-strip sequence.

PAINTED SPECTATORS
The way that painted figures respond to events is an important element in storytelling. Sassetta (below) vividly evokes the townsfolk's fear and curiosity by including a group of female spectators who peer down onto the action.

Gold has rubbed off here and below, revealing red underlayer

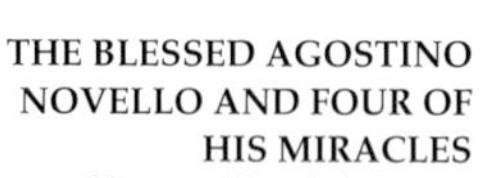

ST. FRANCIS BEFORE THE SULTAN
Sassetta; 1437–44; 34¼ x 20¾ in (87 x 52.5 cm); egg tempera on poplar
This picture and that on the right originate from an altarpiece painted for the church of San Francesco in Borgo Sansepolcro, which included a large painting of St. Francis flanked by eight panels showing scenes from his life. Here, the saint attempts – unsuccessfully – to convert the Sultan of Egypt to Christianity by offering to walk through fire (rendered by gold leaf tooled into flaming arabesques) to prove the power of the Christian faith.

All the panels with scenes from St. Francis's life have the same shape

ST. FRANCIS AND THE WOLF OF GUBBIO
Sassetta; 1437–44; 34¼ x 20¾ in (87 x 52.5 cm); egg tempera on poplar
In another episode from the life of St. Francis, the saint tames a wolf that has been terrorizing the people of Gubbio. Old bones and a dismembered body, gory reminders of the beast's misdemeanors, are scattered nearby. As St. Francis and the wolf shake hands on the agreement that the animal will stop its killing if the townsfolk provide it with food, a notary writes out a contract to that effect. At the town's gate, the men crowd around, keeping a safe distance from the wolf.

THE BLESSED AGOSTINO NOVELLO AND FOUR OF HIS MIRACLES
Simone Martini; c.1324; 78 x 101¼ in (198 x 257 cm); tempera on wood
This image of a monk flying down like Superman to save a child is one of several scenes from an altarpiece dedicated to Agostino Novello. Compressing time, the artist shows the child both during and after his fall. As the mother looks on, Agostino swoops in, catches the offending plank, and blesses the boy, who – once revived – acknowledges his rescuer.

THE FALL OF ICARUS
Pieter Bruegel; c.1555; 29 x 44 in (73.5 x 112 cm)
This appears to be an idyllic pastoral scene: a farmer cuts terraces in his field; a shepherd leans pensively on his crook as his sheep safely graze; a splendid galleon passes by, heading toward a seaside town glowing in the silvery sunset. Bruegel has hidden his story within this peaceful scene. Barely noticeable to the spectator, and unseen by the figures in the painting, Icarus falls into the sea. According to myth, Icarus used artificial wings to escape from prison with his father. Ignoring warnings of flying too close to the sun, however, his wings melted and he fell to his death.

UNSEEN TRAGEDY
Bruegel expected viewers to know the legend of Icarus. By referring to it only minimally, he used the story to make two moral points – that grand ambition is futile, and that man is blind to the world.

THE ARENA CHAPEL
One of the wonders of Western art, Giotto's narrative cycle is perhaps the most moving interpretation of the Christian story ever told in paint. The panels run in chronological order, telling the story of Joachim and Anna (the Virgin Mary's parents) (p.10), the life of the Virgin, and the life of Christ until his Ascension. In each scene, a monumental simplicity of style combines with an expressive emphasis on the human drama.

SANDHAM MEMORIAL CHAPEL
When Mr. and Mrs. J.L. Behrend saw Stanley Spencer's designs for a series of murals based on his experiences during the First World War, they decided to build this chapel to house them. It was to be a memorial to Mrs. Behrend's late brother, Lieutenant Henry Sandham. "What ho, Giotto," Spencer said when he heard of the idea, acknowledging his debt to the Arena Chapel (left). But the murals illustrate Spencer's unique way of combining his personal experience with the Christian story. The dramatic end wall shows the Day of Judgment, when dead soldiers rise from the battlefield and hand in their crosses to Christ.

WHAAM!
Roy Lichtenstein; 1963; 68 x 160 in (172.5 x 406.5 cm); acrylic on canvas
A picture does not always simply tell the story it appears to. Paintings such as this by the Pop artist Roy Lichtenstein take words and images from popular comic strips and make us look at them afresh by placing them out of context and enlarging them to a massive scale. Here, the drama of a fighter pilot's fatal combat is not so much a story as a vehicle for Lichtenstein's use of bold colors, powerful shapes, and, above all, striking design.

Dramatic highlights

WHEN TELLING A STORY, with words or with pictures, the element of drama can be played up or played down. In some cases, such as Fra Angelico's *Mocking of Christ* (p. 20), we have seen how the artist has eliminated the physical and emotional drama from the scene to tell the story in a way that aids quiet meditation. In contrast, the paintings shown on these pages create a powerful dramatic impact through the actions depicted and the way they are presented. Both present a biblical story with bold theatricality: strong contrasts in light and shade – known as *chiaroscuro* (Italian: "light-dark") – exaggerated gestures, daring compositions, and gritty realism all combine to create images that speak with uncompromising directness to the viewer. The stylistic links between these two paintings are clear: Artemisia Gentileschi was a follower of Caravaggio, whose dramatic style, with its powerful use of *chiaroscuro*, had a massive international influence on 17th-century art.

To be "correct," the disciple's far hand should be smaller

EXPRESSIVE REACTION
Gestures are large – none larger than this. The outstretched arms reach back into the gloomy depths of the picture and out toward the viewer.

DRAMATIC INVOLVEMENT
Caravaggio designed his composition with the intention of involving the spectator in the scene. Showing the disciple Cleophas from the back gives the impression that the viewer is watching over his shoulder. And as he begins to rise from his chair, his elbow appears to burst out of the picture – just as the precariously balanced bowl of fruit seems about to topple forward into the real space occupied by the viewer.

The darkness of the setting adds to the air of mystery and ensures that nothing distracts from the drama being enacted

As Cleophas grips the arms of his chair, so heightening the dramatic tension, the viewer is drawn into the scene

The Supper at Emmaus

CARAVAGGIO *c.1600–01; 55½ x 77¼ in (141 x 196 cm)*

This scene shows the resurrected Christ with two disciples, who up to this point thought they were eating with an unknown stranger. Caravaggio depicts the moment when Christ blesses the bread and the shocked disciples suddenly realize that they are in the company of their risen Lord. It is an intensely theatrical portrayal. Christ is center stage, shown as if beneath a spotlight that throws dark shadows on the wall behind Him. His air of calm concentration and his poised hands accentuate the exaggerated, dramatic reactions of the two disciples. One rises from his chair, while the other throws out his arms in amazement. The innkeeper looks on, bemused.

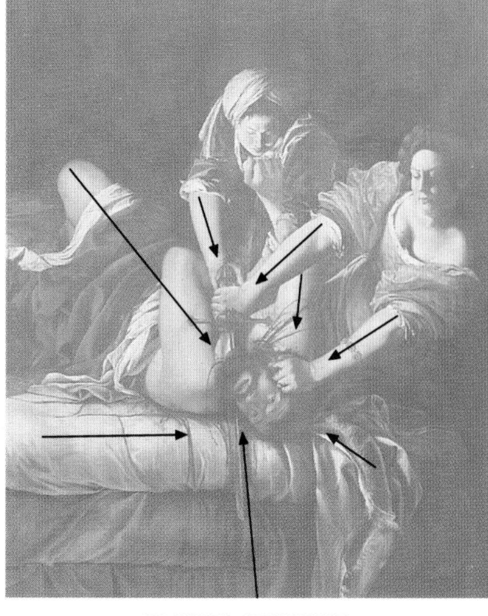

SPOKES OF LIGHT
Like Caravaggio, Gentileschi exploits the dramatic potential of *chiaroscuro* to set a mood and highlight particular elements of the scene. The dark background – appropriate for a scene of seduction and secrecy – concentrates all attention on the action. Broad, bright highlights on arms and legs form spokes of light, which lead inexorably to the horrific focus of the composition: Holofernes's head as it is being severed from his body.

Judith Beheading Holofernes

ARTEMISIA GENTILESCHI

c.1618; 70¾ x 67¾ in (169 x 162 cm)

Judith was a biblical heroine who saved her town from its besiegers. The beautiful widow seduced the Assyrian general Holofernes, got him drunk, and cut off his head with his own sword.
In many versions of this subject, artists chose to show Judith after the beheading, holding Holofernes's head and sword.
It was the dramatic potential of the story, however, that appealed to Gentileschi. She painted it a number of times, here with a particularly gory concentration on the act of the decapitation itself. The spectator is not allowed a sense of safe distance from the horror: as blood spurts forth, the action is pushed, with brutal force, right up against the picture plane.

SENSATIONALIST DETAILS
There is a certain sensationalism in Gentileschi's powerful realism. Judith's face and figure are forcefully modeled by strong lighting from the side, and her brow is creased with grimly determined concentration. A deep shadow accentuates the curve of her cleavage, while the pale skin of her breast is spattered with blood.

PHYSICAL FORCE
Unlike many artists who focused on the heroine's decorative charms, Gentileschi impresses us with the story's violence. Judith's immense physical effort is emphasized: her solid wrists crease as she grips Holofernes's hair and pushes against his head with one hand, sawing at his neck with the other. The detail of the sword handle pressing into Holofernes's flesh is well observed, but disturbingly macabre.

Reading the moral

FAMILY TREE
Though he has squandered his money, the Earl asserts his noble lineage by displaying his family tree. It is this "nobility" that he is selling to the merchant.

WILLIAM HOGARTH'S satirical art shows a completely different approach to storytelling than that of Caravaggio and his followers (pp. 32–33). His interest was in what he called "modern moral subjects." In this narrative series of six paintings, entitled *Marriage à la Mode*, every detail takes part in the moralizing commentary on the main action. The subject under attack is the modern fashion for marriages of convenience between the wealthy middle classes and the impoverished nobility. There are numerous paintings within these paintings: they comment on the action and give warnings of horrors to come. They also reflect the fashion for "foreign" art and artists, against which the English artist Hogarth had a personal vendetta.

The Marriage Contract

WILLIAM HOGARTH
c.1743; 27½ x 35¾ in (70 x 91 cm)
The first painting shows the marriage being arranged between the children of the penniless, and aptly named, Lord Squanderfield and a rich but "common" merchant. This loveless union, based on vanity and profligacy – the exchange of dowry money for a title – is doomed. The bride and groom ignore each other; while the foppish Viscount admires himself in the mirror, his forlorn fiancée receives the attentions of the lawyer Silvertongue. Two fettered dogs symbolize their plight. In the next two scenes (bottom) the newlyweds embark on a life of fashionable debauchery; the Viscount and his young mistress contract venereal disease.

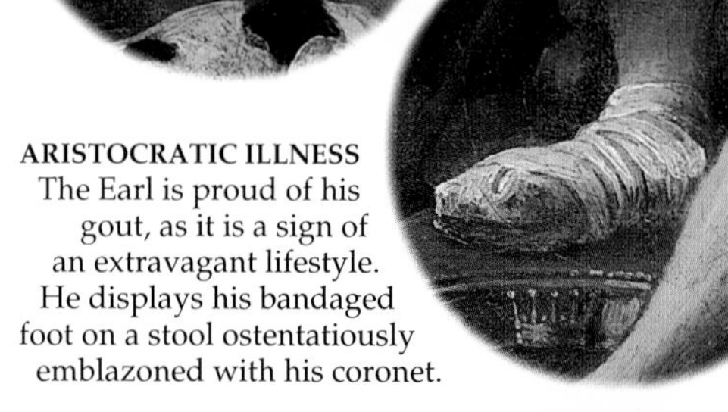

FASHIONABLE FEET
Every detail is loaded with satire. Daintily turned apart, and in French shoes (foreign equaled bad in Hogarth's eyes), the Viscount's feet typify his affected manner.

ARISTOCRATIC ILLNESS
The Earl is proud of his gout, as it is a sign of an extravagant lifestyle. He displays his bandaged foot on a stool ostentatiously emblazoned with his coronet.

THE MARRIAGE CONTRACT
William Hogarth; c.1743; 27½ x 35¾ in (70 x 91 cm)
In the old Earl's aristocratic home, the marriage contract is signed, and the young couple's doom is sealed.

SHORTLY AFTER THE MARRIAGE
William Hogarth; c.1743; 27½ x 35¾ in (70 x 91 cm)
The newlyweds are shown in disarray after a night's debauch (separately): their steward, carrying a pile of unpaid bills, exits in despair.

THE VISIT TO THE QUACK DOCTOR
William Hogarth; c.1743; 27½ x 35¾ in (70 x 91 cm)
Here, the Viscount and his mistress seek treatment for venereal disease. The skull on the table is an indication of death to come.

The Countess' Morning Levée

WILLIAM HOGARTH

c.1743; 27½ x 35¾ in (70 x 91 cm)

Coronets on the bed and mirror indicate that the old Earl has died and his son has inherited the title. The Countess is giving a morning reception. As a French hairdresser attends to her and a female guest swoons at the Italian *castrato*, the Countess attends to Silvertongue. With his feet up on the sofa (he is obviously at home in her boudoir), he invites her to a masked ball – a common place of assignation for lovers. In the final scenes, the Earl discovers his wife with Silvertongue, and is killed; the Countess commits suicide when she reads that her lover has been hanged for her husband's murder.

WATCHING IN HORROR
The mythological figure of Medusa, with her staring eyes and snake-hair, was so hideous that anyone who saw her turned to stone. But in *The Marriage Contract*, this epitome of horror looks aghast at the scene below, signifying the terrible outcome that lies in store. The positioning of the Medusa, directly above the young couple and the lawyer, is no accident.

UNDERSTATED DETAIL
The coral teething ring hanging on the Countess' chair is the only sign until the last painting in the series that she has had a child – who is shown only once, clinging to its dead mother. A black skin patch and a crippled leg indicate the congenital effects of the venereal disease referred to in the third picture.

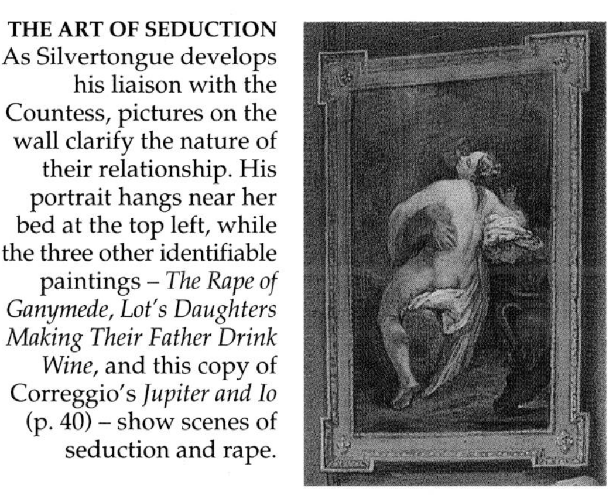

THE ART OF SEDUCTION
As Silvertongue develops his liaison with the Countess, pictures on the wall clarify the nature of their relationship. His portrait hangs near her bed at the top left, while the three other identifiable paintings – *The Rape of Ganymede*, *Lot's Daughters Making Their Father Drink Wine*, and this copy of Correggio's *Jupiter and Io* (p. 40) – show scenes of seduction and rape.

THE SIGN OF THE CUCKOLD
A boy servant unpacks a box of oddments. On a tray, the scene of Leda being seduced by the Swan (Jupiter in disguise) reaffirms Silvertongue's intentions. The horned figure of Actaeon assures us that he will succeed in his seduction: stag horns are the sign of the cuckold – a man whose wife commits adultery.

THE COUNTESS' MORNING LEVEE
William Hogarth; c.1743; 27½ x 35¾ in (70 x 91 cm)
Surrounded by her pretentious entourage, the Countess develops her intimate liaison with the lawyer Silvertongue.

THE KILLING OF THE EARL
William Hogarth; c.1743; 27½ x 35¾ in (70 x 91 cm)
The young Earl has been fatally wounded by his wife's lover – who escapes, seminaked, from a window.

THE SUICIDE OF THE COUNTESS
William Hogarth; c.1743; 27½ x 35¾ in (70 x 91 cm)
As the Countess dies, her miserly father removes her gold ring; suicides forfeited their property.

Variations on a theme

A PAINTING IS NOT simply "about" its identifiable theme: it is about the way the artist expresses that theme in paint. The real meaning of any work of art is communicated through both subject and treatment. Painters may interpret a given subject in an infinite number of ways. Examining variations on the same theme can help us distinguish particular characteristics and heighten our powers of discrimination – which is really what learning to look at paintings is all about. On this page, we see how two roughly contemporary artists expressed totally different artistic visions through the same basic image. Opposite, we discover how two apparently unrelated images, one figurative, one abstract, have surprising links that are not visible at first glance.

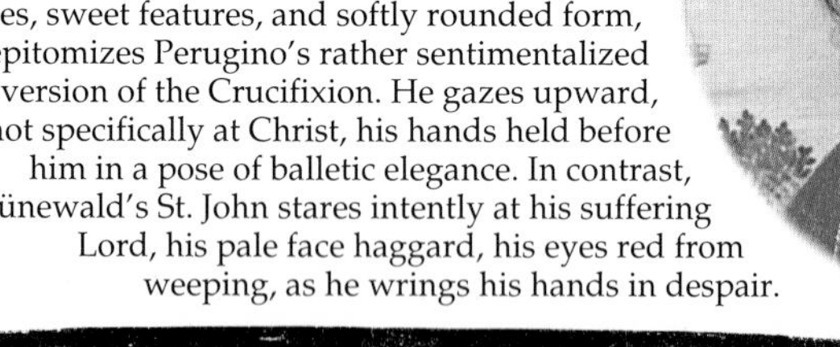

ST. JOHN TRANSFIXED
St. John the Evangelist's face, with its uplifted eyes, sweet features, and softly rounded form, epitomizes Perugino's rather sentimentalized version of the Crucifixion. He gazes upward, not specifically at Christ, his hands held before him in a pose of balletic elegance. In contrast, Grünewald's St. John stares intently at his suffering Lord, his pale face haggard, his eyes red from weeping, as he wrings his hands in despair.

THE SMALL CRUCIFIXION
Matthias Grünewald; c.1520; 24¼ x 18 in (61.5 x 46 cm); oil on wood
The central image of Christian art, the Crucifixion, was a recurrent theme in Grünewald's work. Invariably, he depicted the scene with a gruesome, expressive realism, focusing with terrible intensity on Christ's physical suffering. All is jagged and uncomfortable in this painting; form and color combine to reinforce the feeling of physical and spiritual agony. The sickly pale figure of Christ stands out from the dark background. His emaciated body is twisted, His skin disfigured with wounds, His loincloth torn to shreds. The life is draining out through the emphatic Y-shape of His body, while the arms of the cross droop with His weight – accentuating the sense of downward movement that seems to embody the mood of despair.

THE CRUCIFIXION WITH THE VIRGIN AND ST. JOHN
Pietro Perugino; c.1485; central panel: 39¾ x 22¼ in (101.5 x 56.5 cm)
Despite the obvious similarities in composition, this serene, idealized image could not be further in character from Grünewald's. Instead of the downward movement that dominates the German painting, the eye is led upward toward heaven as Christ transcends His physical suffering. His graceful, virtually unblemished body is dressed in gently billowing drapery and is set – almost floating – against a pale blue sky. Both landscape and figures are depicted with harmonious colors and gentle contours that contrast with the angular forms and eerie colors of Grünewald's version.

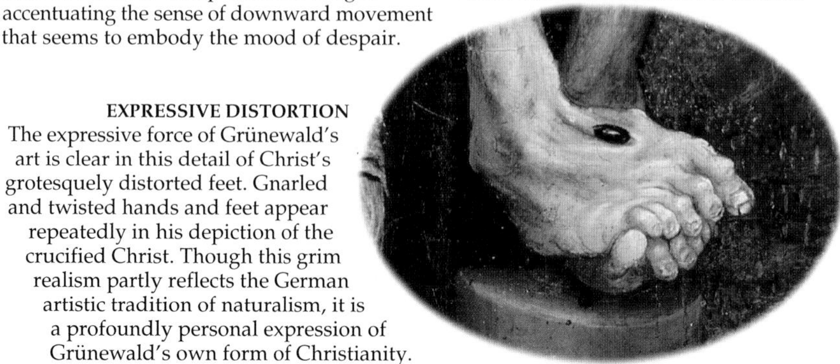

EXPRESSIVE DISTORTION
The expressive force of Grünewald's art is clear in this detail of Christ's grotesquely distorted feet. Gnarled and twisted hands and feet appear repeatedly in his depiction of the crucified Christ. Though this grim realism partly reflects the German artistic tradition of naturalism, it is a profoundly personal expression of Grünewald's own form of Christianity.

THE CREATION OF ADAM

Michelangelo; 1508–12; fresco from the Sistine Chapel ceiling

In this most famous section from the Sistine Chapel, God sweeps down to instill life into Adam – creating the first man. The painting expresses its theme with immense power, using both figurative and abstract means. Figuratively, there is a tremendous sense of vital energy in the depiction of God, His muscles taut beneath His robe, His beard streaming out behind Him, His gaze intent and purposeful. He stretches out to inject energy into Adam, whose physical perfection reflects the fact that he is still "perfect" and untainted by sin. Michelangelo also uses the abstract qualities of composition to evoke the energy of creation, most notably in the way that the outstretched arms are set against empty space so that the fingers almost touch – almost but not quite. It is this gap that creates the effect of vital tension. Across the empty space, the spectator can feel the spark of life-giving energy.

VITAL TENSION

As Adam's hand droops sleepily, the energizing contour of God's forefinger moves in purposefully toward it. If you were to reduce the hands to abstract equivalents, two almost-touching triangles, for example, you would find a similar effect of dynamic tension. If the fingers or triangles touched, the movement would be complete and the sense of tension would be lost.

ADAM

Barnett Newman; 1951–52; 95¾ x 80 in (243 x 203 cm)

Unless you were aware of the title, you might have no idea that this work relates to the Creation of Adam. Its title alerts the spectator to its symbolic language. Newman's abiding preoccupation was with the link between divine and artistic creativity, which he expressed using "shapes and colors ... as symbols," with which he hoped to communicate his ideas to the viewer. The red vertical bands (or "zips," as he called them) have a visual effect similar to the gap in Michelangelo's image, but the zip also embodies a number of symbols. It stands for light, a traditional metaphor for creation; for man (who stood upright, unlike other animals); and it is a phallic symbol of Adam's maleness.

Saints and symbols

SWALLOW
The swallow is one of a number of symbols for the Resurrection of Christ.

THE ART OF THE PAST often contains figures who were immediately recognizable to contemporary viewers and symbols with which they were familiar. Although we may still appreciate such a painting's aesthetic qualities – its style, its use of line and color – the content often remains a mystery. Looking at the religious paintings of western Europe, we repeatedly see the same figures: the Virgin Mary and Christ appear most frequently, but an array of saints and Christian martyrs often accompany them. They may be identifiable by their "attributes" – objects with which they were traditionally shown. Many symbols – of purity, the Resurrection, and so on – also recur in religious art. These may appear as incidental details to the modern eye, but they can hold the key to a painting's particular meaning. Learning how to recognize these visual codes takes a little time and effort, but can greatly deepen our understanding and enjoyment of paintings.

Virgin and Child with St. Jerome and St. Sebastian

CARLO CRIVELLI *c.1490; main panel: 59¼ x 42¼ in (150.5 x 107.5 cm); oil on poplar*

This elaborate altarpiece is known as the *Madonna della Rondine* because of the swallow (*rondine* in Italian) perched on top of the Virgin's throne. A predella, or illustrated base, set with smaller pictures, runs beneath the main image. Three central panels show scenes from the lives of the figures positioned directly above them. Those to the sides show St. Catherine and St. George.

The gourd is balanced on the throne

Embroidered fabric adds to the decorative feel

SYMBOL OF THE RESURRECTION
Like the swallow, the gourd is a symbol of the Resurrection. It was given this meaning because of its role in the story of Jonah – whose re-emergence, unscathed, from the belly of the whale was seen by Christ as a prefiguration of His own death and Resurrection. According to the Bible, God caused a gourd to grow and give shade to Jonah.

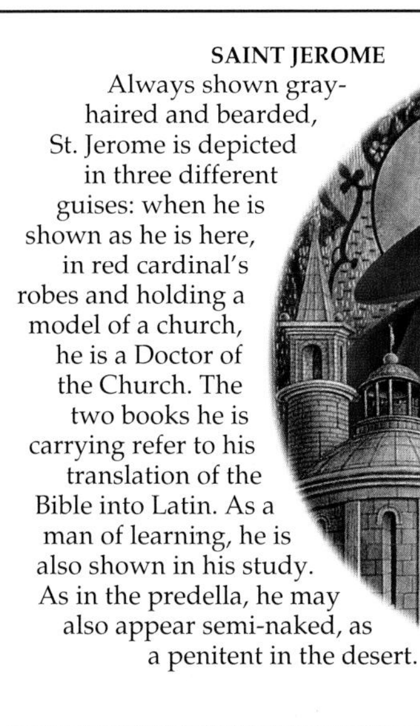

SAINT JEROME
Always shown gray-haired and bearded, St. Jerome is depicted in three different guises: when he is shown as he is here, in red cardinal's robes and holding a model of a church, he is a Doctor of the Church. The two books he is carrying refer to his translation of the Bible into Latin. As a man of learning, he is also shown in his study. As in the predella, he may also appear semi-naked, as a penitent in the desert.

Rays of light burst from the Church

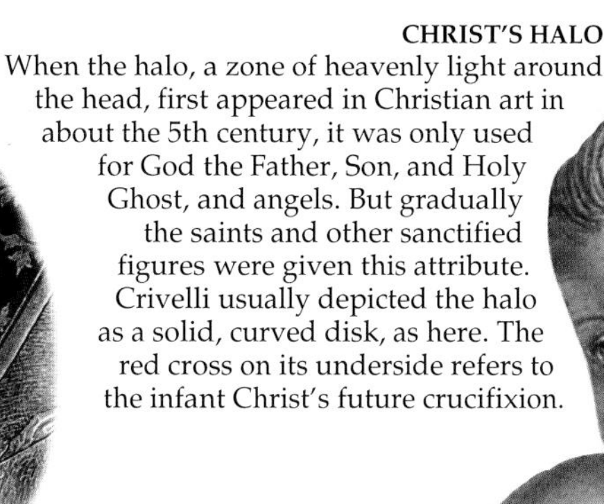

CHRIST'S HALO
When the halo, a zone of heavenly light around the head, first appeared in Christian art in about the 5th century, it was only used for God the Father, Son, and Holy Ghost, and angels. But gradually the saints and other sanctified figures were given this attribute. Crivelli usually depicted the halo as a solid, curved disk, as here. The red cross on its underside refers to the infant Christ's future crucifixion.

Protective coral necklace *(see also p. 7)*

SEBASTIAN'S ARROWS
The depiction of St. Sebastian as a blond youth, elegantly attired in contemporary costume, as he is in the main panel, is unusual. It was much more common to show him as he is in the predella, stripped naked and pierced with arrows (below, and p. 16). The halo signifies his sainthood, but to ensure that the young dandy would be recognized as Sebastian, Crivelli placed a long arrow in his hand (right) and included the corner of a curved bow that juts into the picture at his feet.

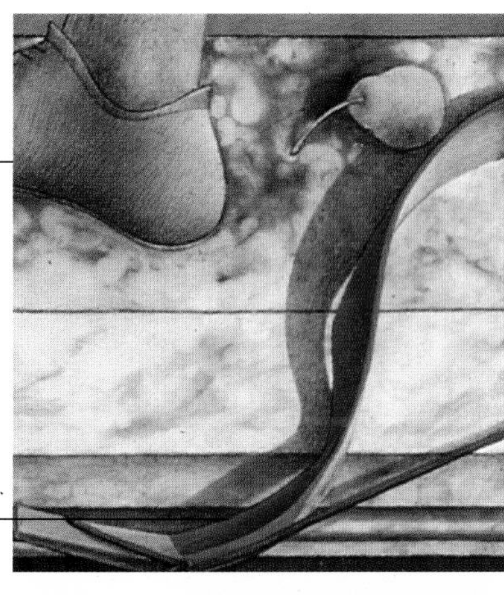

The bow appears to project over the ledge, out into real space

JEROME'S LION
Jerome is usually shown with a red cardinal's hat and a lion – which has been squashed into the composition here. His mane treated in the same linear style as Sebastian's hair, the diminutive beast looks up to the saint, holding out an injured paw. According to legend, Jerome pulled a thorn from the paw of a lion, which then became his devoted friend.

CATHERINE'S WHEEL
Peering sidelong out of the picture, as does Sebastian, the virgin martyr St. Catherine of Alexandria leans decoratively on the instrument of torture that was intended for her death – a wheel, studded with iron spokes. Like Sebastian and the arrows, she survived this attempt on her life. But she was soon beheaded.

MARTYRED SAINT
Directly below Sebastian's image in the main panel, the predella shows the most famous scene associated with the saint. Sebastian, a Roman soldier, was condemned to death for his Christianity. Crivelli gives him the air of an animated puppet, dancing under the arrow blows. This scene (see also p. 16) is usually known, inaccurately, as *The Martyrdom of St. Sebastian*. The saint survived this ordeal, only to be beaten to death and thrown in a sewer.

Literature and legend

OVID'S METAMORPHOSES
Written in the form of a long poem in the first century A.D., Ovid's *Metamorphoses* describe 250 stories in which humans and gods are transformed – metamorphosed – into elements of nature.

APART FROM THE Bible, the text most frequently painted from the Renaissance to the 19th century was Ovid's *Metamorphoses*, a poem retelling fascinating and bizarre ancient myths that concern bodily transformation of some sort – into a tree, cloud, or flower, for example. The *Metamorphoses* were not the only ancient legends popular with artists: stories featuring the heroes involved in the Trojan War also provided a wealth of exciting subject matter. Ancient literature based on these legends, such as the epic poems *The Iliad* and *The Odyssey*, reputedly by Homer, are no longer popular reading matter, and paintings that refer to them are often a mystery. But it is worth becoming familiar with a few of the stories – not just for themselves, but to be able to appreciate how painters have used them.

JUPITER AND IO
Correggio; c.1530; 64¼ x 29¼ in (163.5 x 74 cm)
Jupiter, the ruler of the Roman gods, makes multiple appearances in Ovid's *Metamorphoses* and in art, in the various guises he assumed to carry out his sexual adventures. Here, in an attempt to hide his infidelity with Io from his wife Juno, he has turned himself into a cloud. His face and hand can just be distinguished in the dark gray cloud as he caresses the rapturous nymph. This is only one scene in the story. Other paintings focus on later episodes, such as the one in which Zeus turns Io into a cow to evade their discovery by Juno.

APOLLO AND DAPHNE
Antonio del Pollaiuolo; c.1470; 11½ x 7¾ in (29.5 x 20 cm)
Set in a local Tuscan landscape, with the figures in contemporary dress, this delightful painting illustrates Apollo's hopeless passion for the nymph Daphne. As he tries to force himself on her, her prayer to be saved is answered, and she is transformed into a laurel tree.

LANDSCAPE WITH ECHO AND NARCISSUS
Claude Lorrain; c.1644; 37¼ x 46½ in (94.5 x 118 cm)
Claude sets his mythological figures in an extensive, idealized landscape suffused with the warm glow of the approaching sunset. Punished by Juno, the nymph Echo can speak only the last words she has heard. She loves Narcissus, but he rejects her and falls in love with his own reflection. The nymph fades into a disembodied echo, and the youth pines away for love of his own unattainable image.

METAMORPHOSIS OF NARCISSUS
Salvador Dalì; 1937; 200¾ x 307 in (510 x 780 cm)
The dreamlike strangeness of the Narcissus myth is brilliantly evoked in this Surrealist masterpiece. In the distance, the beautiful young man stands on a pedestal, admiring his own body. As he crouches down to gaze at himself lovingly in the foreground pool, the shape of his body is transformed into the nearby hand. Narcissus's arm becomes a bent finger, his leg and knee become a thumb and thumbnail, and his head is turned into an egg – with a narcissus flower bursting through the shell. At his death, Narcissus was turned into the flower – a transformation omitted from Claude Lorrain's painting (left), but central to Dalì's. Dalì himself wrote that the best way to look at the painting is to stare at the distant figure of Narcissus on the pedestal, until your attention involuntarily switches to other parts of the image.

THE RAPE OF HELEN BY PARIS
Follower of Fra Angelico; c.1450;
20 x 24 in (51 x 61 cm); oil on wood
This animated scene shows the Trojan prince Paris abducting the beautiful Spartan queen Helen – the event that triggered the long and bloody Trojan War. In ancient Greek poems on the theme, Helen was taken by force. In medieval romances, however, she falls in love with Paris and elopes willingly. Here, she appears relatively unperturbed as she is carried off on his back, though one of the other women in the temple looks aghast as Paris's companion makes a grab for her.

ULYSSES DERIDING POLYPHEMUS
J.M.W. Turner; 1829; 57½ x 93 in (146 x 236 cm)
Ulysses's Greek name was Odysseus, and his ten-year journey home to Ithaca after the fall of Troy is the subject of Homer's *Odyssey*. Turner's atmospheric seascape relates to one of the adventures of the ancient Greek hero. He and twelve companions have been trapped in a cave by the one-eyed giant Polyphemus, but escape by getting the giant drunk and blinding him. The blazing dawn that bursts across the sky seems to embody Ulysses's escape from the shadowy darkness of the giant's island.

Painted allegories

PICTURES OFTEN CONTAIN hidden meanings. In allegorical paintings, figures and events are not to be taken at face value: they stand for something else. Renaissance painters, in particular, used characters from classical mythology to personify concepts (love or greed, for example), and set up paintings in which the narrative illustrates a wider moral or philosophical point. Sometimes scholars find contemporary interpretations that can help us "read" the subject matter, but such information is not always available. Trying to unravel the meaning continues to be part of the pleasure of looking at such paintings. A figure's allegorical role may change according to the context. Both pictures featured here include Venus, the goddess of love, but she is used to symbolize two separate aspects of love – lust and beauty.

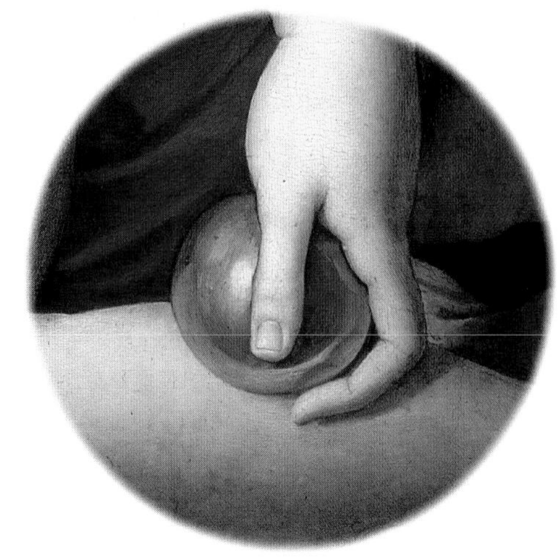

CROSS-REFERENCES
Bronzino's Venus holds the golden apple won in the beauty contest known as the Judgment of Paris (p. 48). One of her rivals in the contest was Minerva, the Roman equivalent of the Greek goddess Pallas Athena, below.

Pallas Expelling the Vices from the Garden of Virtue

ANDREA MANTEGNA *1499–1502; 63 x 75½ in (160 x 192 cm); tempera on canvas*

This painting was commissioned by Isabella d'Este, one of the most intellectual patrons of the Renaissance. It is sometimes known as *The Triumph of Virtue*, a title which sums up its symbolic meaning. The Virtues (three of whom look down from a cloud, while the fourth – Prudence – is imprisoned in a rock) have left the garden of the mind, which has become overrun by Vices. Here, the virtuous goddess of wisdom, Pallas Athena, chases away Venus (symbolizing lust) and the Vices.

The goddess Pallas Athena

GODDESSES AT WAR
Identifiable by her armor, helmet, shield, and spear, Pallas Athena – goddess of both war and wisdom – rushes into the garden, fighting for a just cause. Beside her, around the figure encased in an olive tree, an inscription written in Hebrew and Greek implores, "Come divine companions of the Virtues ... banish these foul monsters of Vices." The goddess is aided by two other virginal companions – the huntress Diana, and Chastity. They run at Venus, who flaunts her sexuality while standing on a centaur, the half man, half horse that symbolizes lust.

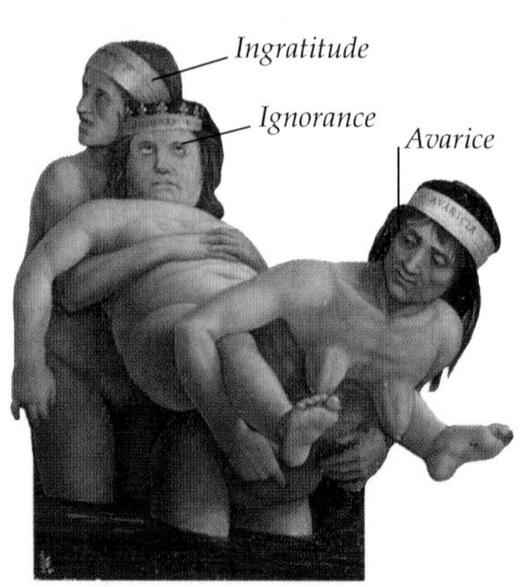

UGLY SINS
Leading the flight from the garden are the Vices Avarice and Ingratitude, who carry the grossly fat, crowned figure of Ignorance between them. Isabella d'Este insisted on keeping tight control of the imagery in her paintings; the use of identifying headbands here was designed to help her guests read the painting's meaning as she intended it to be read.

An Allegory with Venus and Cupid

AGNOLO BRONZINO

c.1545; 57½ x 45¾ in (146 x 116 cm)

Here Venus appears in an erotic allegory that is thought to symbolize unchaste love and its consequences. The precise identification of all the figures in the painting has long been debated, but the central theme is that of Venus using the power of her beauty to disarm her son Cupid, taking his arrow as they kiss. Around the god and goddess are personifications of the results of love.

MOTHER AND SON

Venus was the goddess of love, but the golden apple she holds indicates that she is shown here in the guise of Beauty. Displaying her physical charms to Cupid – and to the spectator – she seduces him with a kiss. Gazing into Venus's eyes, the young god of love is lost in her loveliness, and fails to notice that she is stealing his arrow in which the power of love resides. Love has been robbed of its power by Beauty.

FOLLY AND THE ROSES

The figures in the *Allegory* relate to different aspects of love. As Venus and Cupid kiss, the chubby little boy – representing Folly – prepares to shower the couple with a handful of pink rose petals. He has bells around one ankle, and does not seem to notice the pain (of love) caused by the thorns piercing his foot. Roses were the attribute (p. 38) of Venus because of their beauty, and because their beauty, like love's, hides painful thorns. According to legend, it was drops of blood from Venus's foot that stained white roses red.

LOVE'S PLEASURE AND PAIN

These two figures are thought to represent the results of love. To the right, the distorted, double-sided creature represents the sweetness and pain of pleasure. Pleasure's top half appears as a pretty girl proffering a honeycomb, but her monstrous body ends with a sting in the tail. The tormented figure on the left has been identified as Jealousy, and, more recently, as Syphilis.

TIME REVEALS ALL

The old, winged man with an hour-glass on his back represents Time, who draws back a blue cloak to expose the female figure in the top left-hand corner of the painting. Since her face is a hollow mask, she has been identified as Fraud, although she might also be Oblivion. Two masks lying beside Venus's foot also relate to the goddess's deceitful disarming of Cupid.

Portraits

SECOND IN THE HIERARCHY of the genres (p. 28), after history painting – which has been explored in the previous pages – comes portraiture. While figures in history paintings may be generalized images, portraits provide likenesses of individuals. But great portraiture can provide more than a surface likeness – it can reveal something of the sitter's inner character and spirit. Indeed, we usually do not know whether most of the portraits from the past that we admire are good likenesses: we respond to them because they seem to reveal something about humanity as well as about the individual sitter. Portraits can have many roles, private and public, and their role will affect both the way they are painted and the way they are looked at. A portrait may be a small, intimate picture of a loved one, to be gazed at in private; it may depict the owner of a country estate, and be viewed among other formal family portraits; or it may be a huge portrait of a king, concerned as much with propaganda as with physical likeness.

THE GRESLEY JEWEL
Nicholas Hilliard; 1580–85; 2¾ in (7 cm) diameter; watercolor on vellum
These miniature marriage portraits of Sir Thomas Gresley and his wife Catherine were set in a piece of jewelry. Such portraits were worn as love tokens.

CHARLES I ON HORSEBACK
Anthony van Dyck; c.1638; 144½ x 115 in (367 x 292 cm)
Van Dyck's portrait of Charles I, dressed in armor, with a contemplative, melancholic air, is more than just a likeness. Equestrian portraits have been used since antiquity to show emperors and heroes, and this huge painting of the monarch astride a great steed is an image of kingship – designed to impress Charles's power and authority upon all who saw it.

POPE INNOCENT X
Diego Velázquez; 1650; 55 x 47½ in (139.5 x 120.5 cm)
This remarkable portrait combines breathtaking brushwork with an uncanny sense of vitality and psychological insight. The Pope is shown as if he were holding an audience. Grasping a petition in his left hand, he looks mistrustfully toward Velázquez (a Spanish ambassador as well as an artist).

SELF-PORTRAIT
Rembrandt; c.1665; 45 x 37 in (114.5 x 94 cm)
Rembrandt's self-portraits are considered to be among the most psychologically profound examples of portraiture. Here, he shows himself at work, at the age of about sixty. Areas such as the hands and palette are unfinished, and our eyes are drawn to his aging face as it emerges from the shadows, built up with encrusted *impasto* paint. His eyes meet our gaze with an air of resigned dignity. There is a sense of both time and timelessness quite unlike the almost snapshot quality of Frans Hals's brightly lit portrait below.

THE LAUGHING CAVALIER
Frans Hals; 1624; 33¾ x 27¼ in (86 x 69.5 cm)
His shadow thrown against the wall, the sitter seems to leap out at the viewer with shocking immediacy. The smiles and bravura paintwork (p. 26) in Hals's portraits are often contrasted with Rembrandt's works.

Borrowed poses

In painting portraits, artists sometimes refer to other works of art. Sir Joshua Reynolds used references to the art of classical antiquity to lend an air of heroic nobility to his sitters and to elevate the status of portraiture from mere "face painting."

HERMES
This Greek sculpture from the 4th century B.C. shows similarities to Tarleton's portrait, though Reynolds reversed the pose.

GENERAL SIR BANASTRE TARLETON
Joshua Reynolds; 1782; 103½ x 57¼ in (263 x 145.5 cm)
Reynolds seems to have based the pose of this British war hero (recently returned from the American Revolution) on a celebrated sculpture of the Greek god Hermes, then at Landsdowne House, London.

GIRL IN PROFILE
Gwen John; late 1910s; 18 x 12½ in (46 x 32 cm)
When is a portrait not a portrait? Here, the artist is more concerned with the qualities of color and design than with particular facial features or personality.

Portraits in time

LIKE ALL PAINTINGS, a portrait is a product of its time. Not only is the style characteristic of a particular painter belonging to a particular age, but the sitter also belongs to that specific era – and the fashion of his or her clothes and surroundings gives strong clues to character, taste, and position. Those clues may be lost on the later viewer. The portrait below appears to show an elderly lady doing needlework, but in fact the Countess is wearing modern clothes, has modern furniture, and is engaged in the fashionable society activity of "knotting" (see below.) Reynolds's carefully observed details would have been appreciated by mid-18th-century viewers, just as spectators in the 1970s would have placed Hockney's sitters among the stylish London set.

FASHION FABRIC
Like the dress and cape in the portrait below, this silk fabric was designed in the mid-18th-century. Contemporary viewers of both Reynolds's and Hockney's portraits would have been unconsciously aware of the fashion qualities of the Countess' silk robe, with its distinctive pineapple motif, and of Mrs. Clark's purple-and-pink maxi-dress. Celia Birtwell (Mrs. Clark's maiden name) and Ossie Clark were fabric and fashion designers, so style in Hockney's painting is particularly pertinent.

Anne, Countess of Albermarle

SIR JOSHUA REYNOLDS

c.1760; 49¾ x 39¾ in (127 x 101 cm)

Looking almost warily towards the spectator, the widowed Countess sits with her knotting shuttle in her hands, a wicker basket and scissors resting casually on the modern Chippendale breakfast table beside her. In this intimate portrait of a friend's mother, Reynolds records, in minute detail, her "conservatively fashionable" taste. Her black silk cape and her dress both show fabric patterns in vogue in the mid-1750s, and the cape ends in a froth of fashionable lace at the elbows.

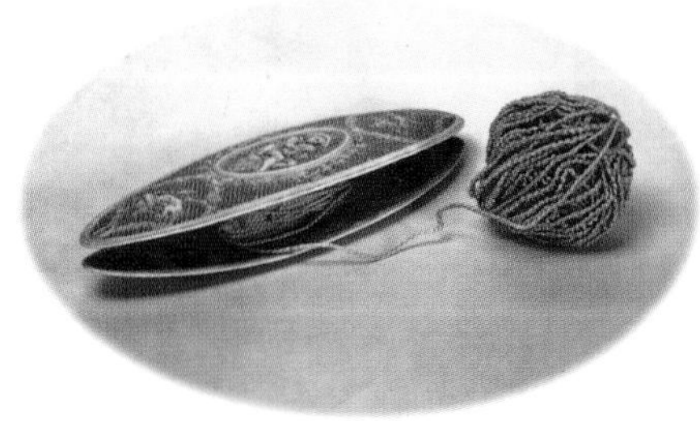

KNOTTING SHUTTLE
This knotting shuttle is similar to the one that the Countess is using. Knotting was a technique whereby thread was made into decorative fringes for dresses or upholstery.

Mr. and Mrs. Clark and Percy

DAVID HOCKNEY *1970–71;*
84 x 120 in (213.5 x 305 cm); acrylic on canvas

This double portrait was painted in Celia Birtwell and Ossie Clark's London home, the year after their marriage – at which the artist had been best man. Painting his friends in their own living room, Hockney has created a strikingly casual, formal portrait. We are still close enough in time to the painting to make its fashion elements appear dated.

DESIGNER CHAIR
Like the straight-lined table, the Clarks' chair, based on this Bauhaus design, was in vogue in the early 1970s.

IN PROGRESS
Hockney captures the effect of light streaming in through the window. Here, he puts the finishing touches to the highlights on Celia's hair.

OSSIE AND THE CAT
The day Hockney arrived to take photographs for the composition, Ossie had just gotten out of bed, and had no shoes on. He was slouched in a chair, smoking, with a white cat on his lap, while Celia stood nearby. This photo has been "squared up" to be enlarged and transferred to canvas.

The nude

THE NUDE HAS BEEN a recurring theme in Western art since classical times, when the ancient Greeks and Romans depicted the naked body in idealized terms. The role and effect of a nude can vary: it can represent an image of harmony and ideal proportion; it can display the technical skill of anatomical drawing; it can express human qualities ranging from vulnerability to anger to joy; and it can be blatantly erotic. Historically, there has long been a divide between the male and the much more prevalent female nude. While the male nude often represents muscular, heroic qualities, the female nude is most often depicted as an object of sensual beauty to be looked at and admired by men. With both sexes, there is usually a difference between the real, naked body and the painted nude. Often, the particulars of a specific model's body are adapted to create a generalized image of what is considered beautiful or to conform to the artist's particular style.

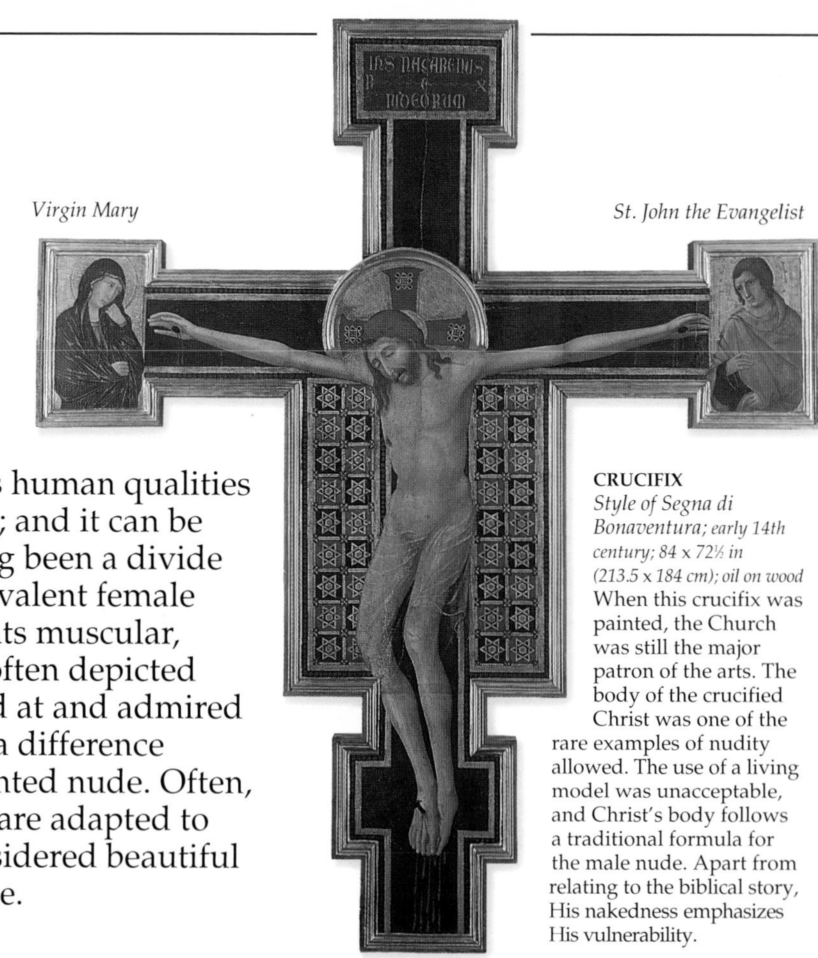

Virgin Mary

St. John the Evangelist

CRUCIFIX
Style of Segna di Bonaventura; early 14th century; 84 x 72½ in (213.5 x 184 cm); oil on wood
When this crucifix was painted, the Church was still the major patron of the arts. The body of the crucified Christ was one of the rare examples of nudity allowed. The use of a living model was unacceptable, and Christ's body follows a traditional formula for the male nude. Apart from relating to the biblical story, His nakedness emphasizes His vulnerability.

CUPID COMPLAINING TO VENUS
Lucas Cranach the Elder; 1530s; 32 x 21½ in (81.5 x 54.5 cm); oil on wood
Images of Venus appeared in Italy in the late 15th century and spread throughout Europe, being popular with collectors of secular (non-religious) art. Here, she ignores her son's complaint about being stung by bees while stealing honey and displays herself to the spectator. This is no ancient goddess, but a sexually enticing contemporary woman; her fashionable hat and necklace accentuate her nakedness.

THE JUDGMENT OF PARIS
Peter Paul Rubens; c.1632–35; 57 x 76¼ in (145 x 193.5 cm); oil on wood
Here, Venus appears in another mythological episode, in which she and two other goddesses, Minerva and Juno, take part in a beauty contest judged by Paris – seen offering Venus the prize of the golden apple. This was a popular subject with artists, partly because it offered the chance to show the female nude at three different angles. Rubens's voluptuous nudes reveal a very different view of female beauty from that seen in Cranach's slim, small-breasted Venus.

LIFE SCHOOL AT THE ROYAL ACADEMY
Johann Zoffany; 1771–72; 47½ x 59½ in (120.5 x 151 cm)
An artist's training traditionally involved acquiring skills in depicting the human body – by studying antique sculptures, anatomy, and painting the nude from life, as illustrated in this scene at the Royal Academy.

EROTIC OR OBSCENE?
The line between eroticism and obscenity can alter. At some point, the owners of Bronzino's *Allegory* (p. 43) found its nudity too sexually explicit. They covered Cupid's bottom with sprigs of leaves, painted out Venus's tongue, and draped her modestly with a loincloth.

LA GRANDE ODALISQUE
Jean-Auguste-Dominique Ingres; 1814; 35¾ x 24½ in (91 x 62 cm)
Exotic surroundings and the sensuous textures of silk, fur, and feathers add to the cool eroticism of this famous nude. The image of an odalisque, or female slave, lounging in some oriental harem, had a widespread sexual appeal and was a particularly popular nude subject. Here we can see how the artist has altered the shape of the human body to create what he considered a more ideal form. To "improve upon" nature, Ingres has added two extra vertebrae to elongate the odalisque's spine. The result is to extend the curve of her back as she turns to look at the spectator over her marble-smooth shoulder.

RECLINING NUDE WITH NECKLACE
Pablo Picasso; 1968; 44¾ x 63¾ in (113.5 x 161.5 cm)
While the distortion of the human body is not obvious in Ingres's nude, it is the most immediately apparent aspect of Picasso's picture, probably of his second wife, Jacqueline. Not only are her features simplified and expressively distorted, but Picasso has included her buttocks, genitals, and breasts in the same view, accentuating the powerful sexuality of her body. She is painted in "unnatural" vibrant colors of red, green, blue, white, and yellow, with a variety of brushstrokes that retain an extraordinary sense of energy. By contrast, her calm expression heightens the frenzy of the paint.

Landscapes

ALTHOUGH LANDSCAPE PAINTINGS have existed since ancient times, when pastoral scenes adorned the walls of villas, the history of landscape in Western art is an intermittent one. With certain significant exceptions, the painted landscape during the Renaissance was usually an element in religious, mythological, or portrait paintings (pp. 7, 16, & 60), rather than the main subject. It was not until the 17th century that landscape attained wide-spread popularity in its own right. By the 19th century it had become one of the most dominant forms of art. When we look at painted landscapes, we may imagine artists sitting out in the countryside painting what they see in front of them. But up until the end of the last century, even though some artists made sketches from nature, finished landscapes were virtually always composed and painted indoors. Even those painted directly from nature do not present a mirror image of the world: the artist's response, selectivity, and style all work to transform nature into art.

THE ARNO VALLEY
These similar details of a winding river appear in the backgrounds of a religious painting and a mythological painting by Antonio and Piero del Pollaiuolo (pp. 16 & 40). They both show the River Arno near Florence, where the brothers lived and worked in the 15th century.

A LANDSCAPE WITH A RUINED CASTLE AND A CHURCH
Jacob van Ruisdael; 1665–70; 43 x 57½ in (109 x 146 cm)
The influential landscape painter Ruisdael infused his landscapes with a powerful sense of mood that is clearly seen in this panorama, with its dark, brooding sky. Though the flat horizon is characteristic of the local Dutch landscape, the view is imaginary, with the spire piercing the skyline and the crumbling ruin included for compositional and dramatic effect.

CORNARD WOOD
Thomas Gainsborough; 1748; 48 x 61 in (122 x 155 cm)
This early "schoolboy" landscape seems to relate to a description by Joshua Reynolds of Gainsborough's method of making models "composed of broken stones, dried herbs, and pieces of looking glass, which he magnified and improved into rocks, trees, and water." Looking carefully, we see a number of "unnatural" elements. The water reflects nonexistent branches, and though the artist uses the common device of leading the eye into the distance along a winding road, the figures placed on the road are tiny and inconsistently scaled.

DEDHAM FROM LANGHAM

John Constable; c.1812–13; 5¼ x 7½ in (13.5 x 19 cm); oil on canvas laid on board

Constable's landscapes are often described as "revolutionary" because he looked directly to nature for his inspiration, aiming to capture the ever-changing light and atmosphere of the English countryside. This delightful small sketch is one of numerous studies he made in the open air. To the 20th-century eye, its free, fluid brushstrokes and vivid, economical evocation of a breezy late-summer day (it is dated August 24) may have as much appeal as the huge, highly finished "six footers" such as the *Hay Wain* (p. 61), painted in his studio for exhibition. The rapidly applied flick and blob of paint in the foreground is a resting cow. It adds an effective flash of white against the green, and makes a powerful visual link with Dedham Church in the distance.

Roughly cut canvas

Friedrich designed the frame for his "landscape altarpiece," including religious imagery such as angels

THE CROSS IN THE MOUNTAINS

Caspar David Friedrich; 1808; 45¼ x 43½ in (115 x 110.5 cm)

The German Romantic artist Caspar David Friedrich found spiritual inspiration in the contemplation of nature and imbued his landscapes with a mystical intensity. Here, he has even used a landscape as the basis for an altarpiece, setting the crucified Christ on a rocky, fir-dotted mountain top, with a reddening sky that is split by three broad shafts of light. This startlingly unconventional altarpiece caused a furor among artistic circles when it was first exhibited in 1808. One critic commented that it would be "a veritable presumption, if landscape painting were to sneak into the church and creep onto the altar."

MONT SAINTE-VICTOIRE

Paul Cézanne; 1904–06; 29 x 35¾ in (73.5 x 91 cm)

In this late work by Paul Cézanne, overlapping patches of color construct the rugged limestone mountain and the wooded landscape beneath it. Cézanne began painting landscapes in the open air with his Impressionist colleague Camille Pissarro (p. 29), but his art moved away from the Impressionist aim of capturing fleeting surface effects. He sought to depict the underlying forms and spatial relationships of nature. "Passionately fond of the contours" of Provence, he was obsessed with Mont Sainte-Victoire (left), which he painted some 60 times.

Still life

OF ALL THE GENRES, still life has generally been considered the least "significant." Yet still life has always been among the most commercially popular forms of art. The English term "still life" comes from the Dutch *stilleven*, meaning "motionless nature." The focus is on an arrangement of inanimate objects – anything from cut flowers to a skull, though the artist may include living creatures, as van Huysum (right) and Matisse (p. 53) have done. Artists of different countries and centuries have concentrated on different aspects of still life. In 17th-century Holland, for example, still-life objects were used symbolically. Later artists were often primarily interested in exploring the more painterly concerns of composition and color.

STILL-LIFE DETAIL
Sometimes a still life can be just a small part of a much larger painting. This brilliantly painted basket of fruit is shown almost toppling off the table in Caravaggio's *Supper at Emmaus* (p. 32).

EXQUISITE TEXTURES
Van Huysum achieved an extraordinary surface finish, as in the bloom and blemishes on the grapes. The delicately painted butterfly is one of several living creatures included.

FLOWERS IN A TERRACOTTA VASE
Jan van Huysum; 1736–37; 52½ x 36 in (133.5 x 91.5 cm)
The vogue for Dutch flower painting in the 17th and 18th centuries reflects Holland's leading role in horticulture. Van Huysum was unusual in that he painted from nature, rather than from botanical studies. This picture contains flowers that bloom in different seasons; the artist worked on it in both 1736 and 1737.

STILL LIFE: AN ALLEGORY OF THE VANITIES OF HUMAN LIFE
Harmen Steenwyck; 1640–50; 15½ x 20 in (39 x 51cm)
In this still life, all the objects are also symbols, and the painting is laden with hidden meanings. One symbol is probably recognized as rapidly today as it was in 17th-century Holland: the skull, an unmistakable reference to death. But other less obvious symbols make sense of the painting as a "vanitas," or reminder of the vain emptiness of worldly things. The shell, then an exotic rarity, symbolizes wealth; musical instruments and the wine flask represent sensual pleasures; the books, knowledge; the sword, power. Counterbalancing these objects, the watch, the extinguished lamp, and the skull remind viewers that whatever wealth, knowledge, power or pleasure they enjoy, time passes and one day they must die.

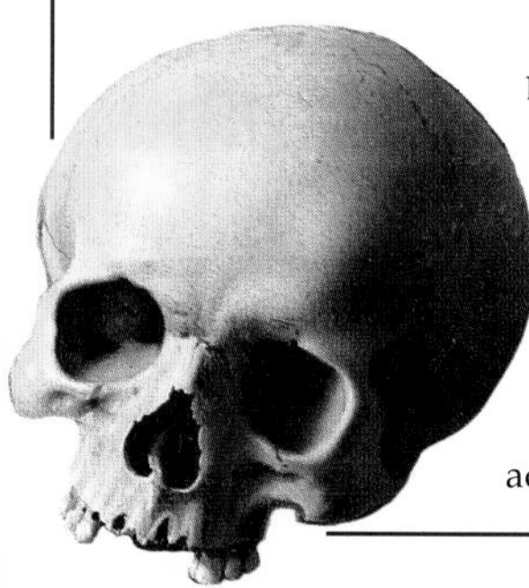

DEATH'S-HEAD
The inclusion of a human skull in a painting is almost always a *memento mori*, or reminder of death. In a "vanitas" picture such as this, the reminder of the transience of human life is used to put human achievements in perspective.

APPLES AND ORANGES
Paul Cézanne; 1895–1900; 28¾ x 36¼ in (73 x 92 cm)
In this splendid still life, Cézanne creates a powerful sense of tension in the obviously artificial arrangement – objects appear to be slipping off the table, and are distorted, because they are shown from shifting viewpoints. Unlike the hyper-real illusionism (p. 18) of the Dutch artists on the previous page, Cézanne stressed the difference between three-dimensional reality and a flat painting. He called works such as this "constructions after nature."

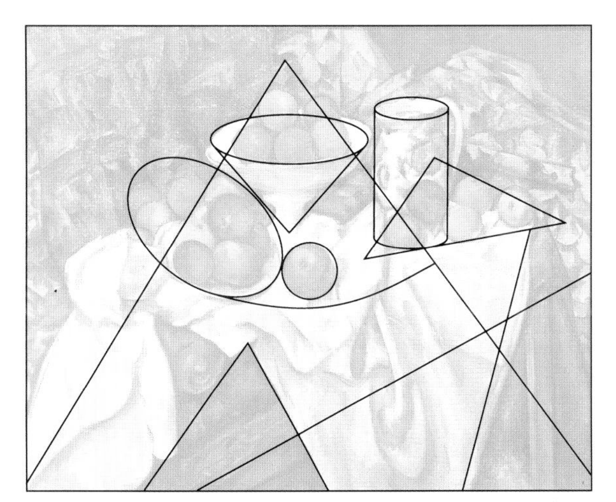

HIDDEN GEOMETRY
Cézanne once said, "See in nature the cylinder, the sphere, and the cone," and his compositions often have a strong geometric basis. In addition to the obvious spherical forms of the apples and oranges, the painting has an underlying geometry. Here, some of the basic shapes have been indicated. They help to tie the objects together and provide a sense of structural stability within the painting.

STILL LIFE WITH GOLDFISH
Henri Matisse; 1911; 58 x 38½ in (147 x 98 cm)
Matisse's aim was to create "an art of balance, of purity and serenity, devoid of ... disturbing subject matter ... something like a good armchair in which to rest." Looking at this still life the viewer can enjoy a pure, soothing sense of visual harmony. Forms are simplified and distorted to create a unified, expressive design, while the luminous orange of the goldfish sings out amid greens and pinks.

Painter and patron

THE DONOR'S SHIELD
In Crivelli's altarpiece (p. 38), one of the donors ensured that his expenditure was acknowledged by having his family's coat of arms included.

WE ARE sometimes able to tell not only who painted a picture, but also for whom they painted it, and why. Just as artists signed their work, so donors might stipulate that some sign of their "ownership" be shown. However, identifying even the authorship of a painting is not always easy. When we have no authenticated signature or documentary evidence to firmly associate a work with a particular painter, the painting may be "attributed to" rather than "by" a given artist. For centuries, artists ran workshops with apprentices and other assistants, and even if the painting has an authentic signature, it may be the product of the workshop, approved and signed – but not necessarily painted – by the master.

THE ABBE SCAGLIA ADORING THE VIRGIN AND CHILD
Anthony van Dyck; 1634–35; 42 x 47¼ in (106.5 x 120 cm)
Here, the donor features prominently, kneeling in front of a silken-robed Madonna whose facial features appear too specific to be anything but a portrait. Indeed, she has been identified as Christina of Savoy, daughter of King Henry IV of France. The Abbé Scaglia, a priest and diplomat, had lost favor with the House of Savoy because of his anti-French sympathies, and was eager to regain their confidence. This would explain why he commissioned a flattering portrait of Christina as the Virgin, to whom he shows himself devoted. Sadly for the Abbé, such flattery got him nowhere.

A MAN IN A TURBAN
Jan van Eyck; 1433; 10 x 7½ in (25.5 x 19 cm)
This small masterpiece is thought by some to be a self-portrait, partly because of the direction of the sitter's glance – which accords with the artist looking in a mirror. But identification is not certain, since portraits known not to be self-portraits also have sitters looking in this direction. The identification of the painter, however, is established – through stylistic links with van Eyck's other works, and because of the inscription on the frame (below).

REVEALING WORDS
The top inscription reads "As I can," and may be a punning reference to a Flemish proverb: "As I (Eyck) can, but not as I (Eyck) would." The bottom reads "Jan van Eyck made me, 21 October 1433."

THE BAPTISM OF CHRIST
Andrea del Verrocchio; c.1470;
70¾ x 59¾ in (180 x 152 cm); tempera on wood
This is one of the few paintings to be attributed with some certainty to Verrocchio's own hand. Although he ran one of the largest artists' workshops in Florence in the 1470s and trained major painters such as Leonardo da Vinci and Perugino (p. 36), he was primarily a sculptor, and details about his paintings are uncertain. For this painting, Verrocchio invited the young Leonardo to paint the left-hand angel, which is clearly distinguishable from the rest of the work. According to the Renaissance artist and art historian Giorgio Vasari, the master was overcome by his apprentice's genius, and "never touched colors again, so ashamed was he that the boy understood their use better than he did."

A DIFFERENT HAND
Although these two angels have aspects in common – such as a delicacy of contour and expression – we can immediately see differences. Only Leonardo's angel, on the left, shows the exquisitely subtle blurring of lines that characterizes his work.

The master and his workshop

Andrea del Verrocchio ran a large and busy workshop, producing sculpture and goldsmith's work as well as paintings. Like other artists' workshops, Verrocchio's employed a number of apprentices and trained painters who worked with the master as assistants and collaborators. Apprenticeships lasted from two to eight years (with an average of four), during which time the apprentice would graduate from perhaps sweeping floors to learning to draw, to grinding colors for the paintings – eventually learning enough artistic skills to be involved in the actual painting. Among Verrocchio's apprentices was Leonardo da Vinci; in the early 1470s, he was allowed to paint a section of his master's *The Baptism of Christ* (above).

PORTRAIT OF A WOMAN
Robert Campin; c.1420–30;
16 x 11 in (40.5 x 30 cm); oil on wood
Without documentary evidence, identifying an artist with a work is fraught with problems. This lovely portrait of an unknown woman is said to be by Robert Campin, a leading painter who ran a large workshop in Tournai (now in Belgium) in the early 15th century. Unfortunately, no documents have been discovered linking Campin with any particular painting. But art historians now associate him with a group of works, including this one, originally attributed to the "Master of Flémalle". Today, the Master of Flémalle is generally agreed to be Robert Campin.

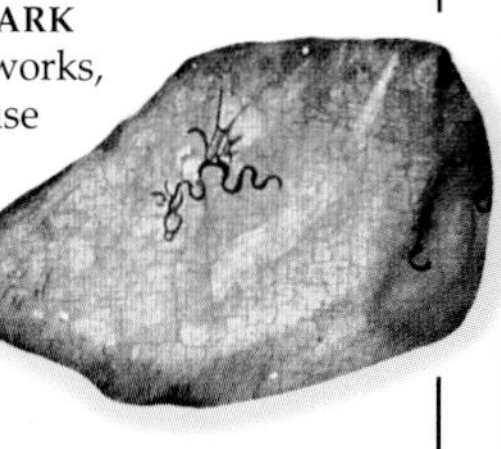

THE ARTIST'S TRADEMARK
Not all artists sign their works, and those who do may use a "device" rather than their name. Cranach's paintings (p. 48) are signed with a winged dragon, based on his family coat of arms.

Changing names

THE WORKSHOP TRADITION of training, in which painters learned from and collaborated with their masters, led to close similarities in style. Indeed, paintings by members of the workshop are often confused with paintings by the master himself (very few women ran their own workshops), and it is not uncommon for attributions to change. Establishing who actually painted a picture, or who was responsible for most of it, depends on many things. Documents and technical analysis are important for determining the date, the techniques used, and so on. But the most important tools are the eyes. It is by scrutinizing details of color, brushwork, subject matter, and treatment, and comparing them with firmly attributed works that art historians can ascribe a painting to a particular painter.

GIRL LEANING ON A WINDOWSILL
Rembrandt; 1645; 32 x 26 in (81.5 x 66 cm)
The authenticity of this painting by Rembrandt has not been questioned. The girl leans casually on a sill, fingering her necklace as she gazes out at the viewer. It may have been a variant of this picture that van Hoogstraten painted (left) when he was a pupil in Rembrandt's workshop. If so, Rembrandt may have supervised that work, perhaps adding a few finishing touches and even signing it.

Rembrandt's shrinking oeuvre

At the beginning of the 20th century, Rembrandt's surviving output was thought to consist of some 988 paintings: experts now attribute fewer than 300 to his hand. Many of Rembrandt's masterpieces have been re-attributed to his pupils. But without "proof," attribution remains a matter of opinion, albeit expert, and one person's Rembrandt may be another's van Hoogstraten, or Fabritius, or Drost – to name a few of the artists now thought to have painted many of the pictures once attributed to their master.

GIRL AT AN OPEN HALF-DOOR
Rembrandt or Samuel van Hoogstraten; 1645; 40¼ x 33 in (102 x 84 cm)
This picture is one of the most famous "Rembrandts" currently held in the United States. Signed "Rembrandt f. 1645," it is labeled in the Art Institute of Chicago – where it hangs – as being painted by Rembrandt. But in a major Rembrandt exhibition of 1991–92, it was "attributed to Samuel van Hoogstraten." Among the reasons for this change are the facts that the pose is stiffer and the surface smoother than is usual with Rembrandt.

LOOKING CLOSELY
With its subtle shading and softly modeled features, the girl's face shows strong similarities to a van Hoogstraten self-portrait also painted in 1645.

PORTRAIT OF AN OLD MAN WITH A BOY
Tintoretto or Marietta Robusti; c.1585; 40½ x 32¾ in (103 x 83.5 cm)
In 1920, it was discovered that this major work attributed to Tintoretto was signed with the monogram of his daughter, Marietta Robusti. However, not all scholars accept that it is by her. Robusti was a renowned member of her father's extensive workshop until she died in childbirth at the age of about 30. The decline in Tintoretto's output after her death is usually ascribed to his grief – but it may be a measure of her productivity in the workshop.

THE CAROUSING COUPLE
Judith Leyster; 1630; 26¾ x 21¾ in (68 x 55 cm)
This work was sold to the Louvre as a Frans Hals in 1893, but a monogram showed it to be by one of his followers, Judith Leyster. A change of name affects how commercially and artistically valuable a painting is considered to be: a male critic noted that looking at Leyster's Hals-like works, we "detect the weakness of the feminine hand." We look at paintings with expectations and prejudices, not just with our eyes.

Original or fake?

The most significant change of authorship a painting can undergo is when it is revealed as a forgery. In 1947, the art world was shocked to discover that *Supper at Emmaus*, thought to be one of the most important paintings by Jan Vermeer, was a fake, painted in the 1930s. Perception of the picture's greatness altered.

CHRIST IN THE HOUSE OF MARTHA AND MARY
Jan Vermeer; 1654–55; 63 x 55¾ in (160 x 142 cm)
Vermeer is only known to have created this one biblical painting before turning to genre scenes (pp. 18 & 28). In the 1930s, there was much speculation about the possible existence of other Vermeers on religious themes. The forger Han van Meegeren fed the art market with what it was expecting to find (far right).

THE SUPPER AT EMMAUS
Han van Meegeren; c.1937; 50¾ x 46 in (129 x 117 cm)
Van Meegeren made his "Vermeer" show the influence of Caravaggio (p. 32), in accordance with expectations about Vermeer's religious works. It was accepted as authentic, and bought by the Boymans Museum of Rotterdam for almost $300,000. Once the forgery was revealed, it was removed from the wall. In response to public demand, however, it was rehung – but without an identifying label.

Another language

So far we have focused almost exclusively on Western art, but it is important to remember that every culture has its own artistic tradition. Just as we cannot see a Renaissance painting with the same eyes as a Renaissance viewer, so we can never see an Aboriginal painting in the same way as an Aboriginal Australian. Aboriginal art centers on the "Dreaming": the state of reality beyond the everyday, which encompasses social and spiritual laws as well as the many creation myths that focus on the activities of sacred ancestors, such as the kangaroo featured in this painting. Although it may appear and appeal to Western eyes as an abstract image, the painting uses graphic symbols to tell a Dreaming story. According to Aboriginal law, only members of the artist's kinship group with the right to possess the secret knowledge this painting embodies can fully appreciate its significance. But it is still possible for all of us to enjoy and appreciate it at some level. There is no such thing as a "right" way to look at any painting, for we all engage in the silent dialogue in our own unique way.

Kangaroo Dreaming

MICHAEL NELSON TJAKAMARRA

1992; 57½ x 39¼ in (46 x 100 cm); acrylic on canvas.

As well as its wider meaning (see left), the term "Dreaming" can also refer to specific narratives relating to the creation myths. Like most Aboriginal art, this picture relates to the artist's spiritual ancestry. The painting combines traditional graphic symbols, which have been used for thousands of years, with the modern medium of acrylic on canvas, which has only been used by Aboriginal artists from the central deserts of Australia since 1971. The symbols have a variety of meanings, and the artist may explain the painting in numerous ways, choosing a level he considers appropriate for the viewer. Members of the artist's kinship group may be told its deeper meanings, but the public can only be told that it tells the Dreaming story of the kangaroo traveling across the land from sacred site to sacred site.

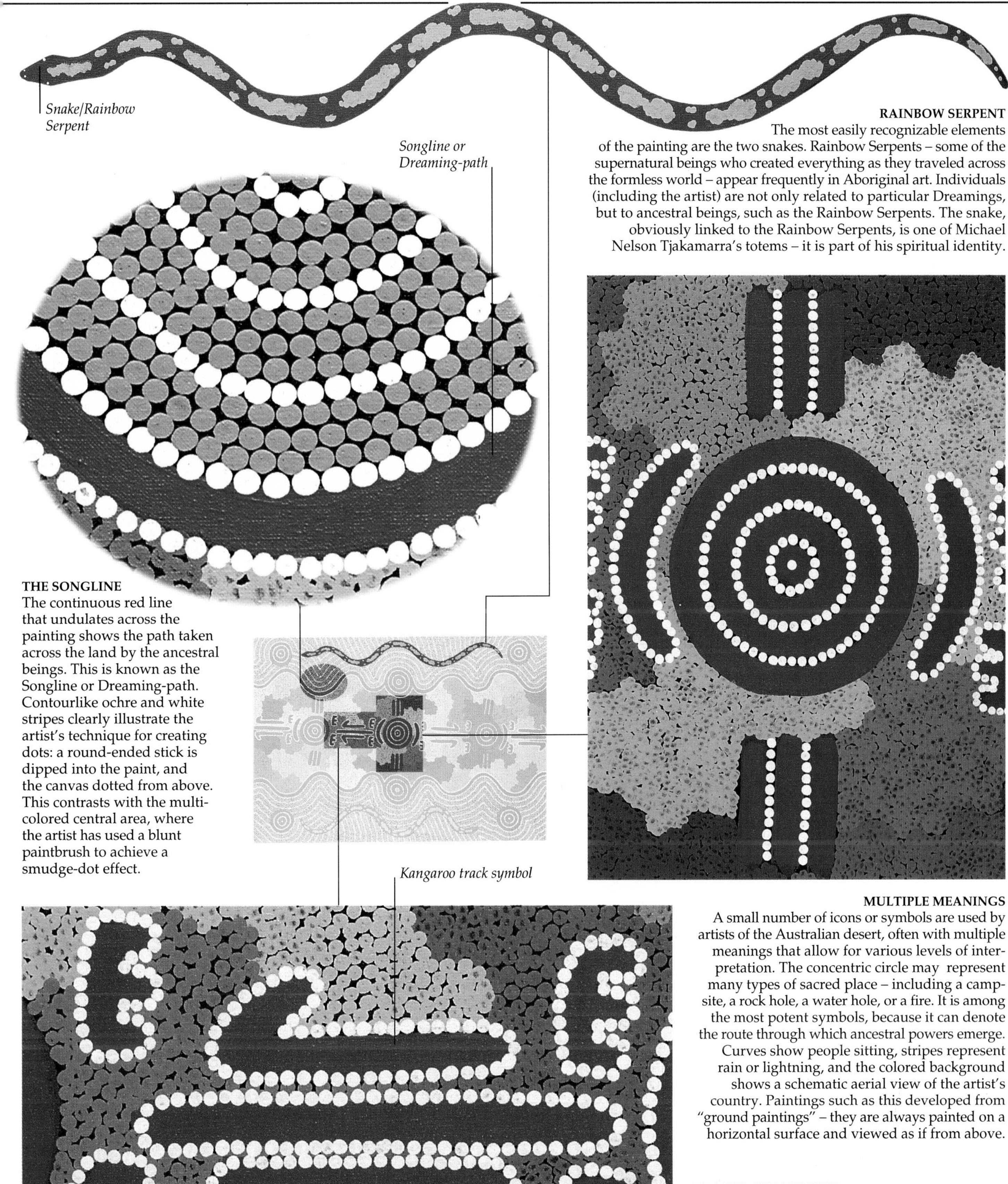

RAINBOW SERPENT
The most easily recognizable elements of the painting are the two snakes. Rainbow Serpents – some of the supernatural beings who created everything as they traveled across the formless world – appear frequently in Aboriginal art. Individuals (including the artist) are not only related to particular Dreamings, but to ancestral beings, such as the Rainbow Serpents. The snake, obviously linked to the Rainbow Serpents, is one of Michael Nelson Tjakamarra's totems – it is part of his spiritual identity.

THE SONGLINE
The continuous red line that undulates across the painting shows the path taken across the land by the ancestral beings. This is known as the Songline or Dreaming-path. Contourlike ochre and white stripes clearly illustrate the artist's technique for creating dots: a round-ended stick is dipped into the paint, and the canvas dotted from above. This contrasts with the multi-colored central area, where the artist has used a blunt paintbrush to achieve a smudge-dot effect.

MULTIPLE MEANINGS
A small number of icons or symbols are used by artists of the Australian desert, often with multiple meanings that allow for various levels of interpretation. The concentric circle may represent many types of sacred place – including a campsite, a rock hole, a water hole, or a fire. It is among the most potent symbols, because it can denote the route through which ancestral powers emerge. Curves show people sitting, stripes represent rain or lightning, and the colored background shows a schematic aerial view of the artist's country. Paintings such as this developed from "ground paintings" – they are always painted on a horizontal surface and viewed as if from above.

TRACKS AND TOTEMS
Tracks of kangaroo ancestors moving across the desert are shown by a long line flanked by two arrow shapes – which correspond to the marks left by the animal's legs, feet, body, and tail. The E-shaped symbol represents meat and can signify a variety of different animals that can be hunted. Like the snake, the kangaroo is one of the artist's totems.

From museum to merchandise

REMBRANDT PLATE
Rembrandt's huge masterpiece of group portraiture, *The Night Watch*, has been reduced in size and stature to become a glossy plate decoration.

PAINTINGS ARE not only reproduced in books, magazines, on television, and in videos; they adorn T-shirts, note cards, address books, and a multitude of other merchandise. Throughout history, painters have often deliberately referred to well-known works by other artists: such allusions set a painting in the context of a recognized artistic language and add to its layers of meaning. However, when a painting becomes the basis of a textile design or a cheese advertisement, its unique nature is transformed. It could be argued that merchandising increases public awareness of paintings, and makes them more accessible. But the irony is that paintings treated in this way may become so familiar as designs that it becomes difficult to look at them afresh as actual paintings.

MONA LISA (LA GIOCONDA)
Leonardo da Vinci; c.1503–06; 30¼ x 20¾ in (77 x 53 cm)
Leonardo's portrait of an unknown woman, often identified with Lisa Gherardini, wife of a wealthy Florentine merchant, is probably the most famous painting in Western art. Yet its fame and familiarity make the viewer less likely to look closely or appreciate the originality of its subtle naturalism. For many, it is simply a "must see" image to be ticked off on the tourist itinerary.

RINALDO AND ARMIDA
Angelica Kauffmann; 1772; 50½ x 40¼ in (128 x 102.5 cm)
This scene from an epic Italian poem shows the Christian prince Rinaldo enraptured by the sorceress Armida. It is painted by one of the most successful pre-20th-century female artists, Angelica Kauffmann, a Neo-Classical painter whose fame and popularity was spread through the countless prints that were made of her works. Both paintings and prints inspired numerous works of decorative art, from snuffboxes and vases, to painted furniture and domestic interiors.

DECORATIVE INSPIRATION
The design on this 19th-century pot was inspired by Kauffmann's *Rinaldo and Armida*. Her friend Sir Joshua Reynolds argued that using designs from fine art for decorative art could "infuse into those lower departments a style and elegance, which will raise them far above their natural rank."

Duchamp's signature

REPLICA OF L.H.O.O.Q.
Marcel Duchamp; 1941–42; 7½ x 4¾ in (19 x 12 cm); collotype and watercolor
One of the most influential artists of the 20th century, Duchamp challenged accepted values of art and taste and the idea that a work of art had to be "unique." Among his most provocative works is this version of Leonardo's *Mona Lisa*. Choosing a painting that had become the object of near-religious reverence, he took a reproduction of the portrait, defaced it with a mustache and beard, and wrote the letters L.H.O.O.Q. beneath it. Pronounced in French, these letters spell out an obscene phrase.

The fine art of merchandise

Rather than enjoying paintings in art galleries, many people are more likely to look at them almost inadvertently, on postcards, playing cards, book covers, and as product decorations. The vogue for "merchandising" paintings is bound up with with the need to create extra revenue for museums and art galleries, as well as the idea of making art more accessible to the general public. For some, paintings are seen almost as a kind of attractive packaging, but for others such merchandising may trigger an interest in looking at paintings in the original. After seeing the merchandise, experiencing the real thing can come as a revelation.

EXOTIC DRESS
Inspired by Gauguin's colorful paintings of Tahiti, this dress design includes copies of a number of his works, set against a decorative backdrop of tropical flowers. Part of Gauguin's appeal is the harmonious exoticism of his work, which itself often has a strong decorative element. Looking at this dress, do you think it degrades, or simply celebrates the original?

THE WHITE HORSE
Paul Gauguin; 1898; 55¼ x 36 in (140 x 91.5 cm)
One of the paintings reproduced on the dress, this idyllic South Seas island scene shows a white horse – tinted green by the reflections from tropical foliage – drinking in the orange and blue water of a mountain stream while naked horsemen ride nearby. Gauguin's use of flat, unshaded areas of color in this painting make it an easy design to print on textiles.

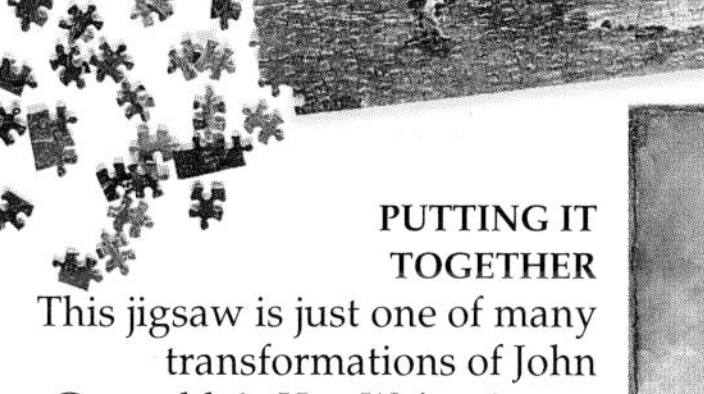

PUTTING IT TOGETHER
This jigsaw is just one of many transformations of John Constable's *Hay Wain* – it was even used in an advertisement for English cheese. Piecing together the jigsaw may increase familiarity with the image, but it is a very different experience from seeing the nearly two-metre (six-foot) painting in reality.

THE HAY WAIN
John Constable; 1821; 51¼ x 72¾ in (130 x 185 cm)
Though Constable painted this picture in his London studio, it is based on studies he made on the River Stour as it passes by the house of his neighbor, Willy Lot. Now known as *The Hay Wain*, it was called *Landscape: Noon* by the artist. In the heat of midday, the horses cool off, and the wheels of the haycart are given a soaking in the water, while an inquisitive dog looks on. An icon of Englishness, Constable's landscape has come to represent the unhurried rural world of a bygone era.

Glossary

Abstract art Art that does not attempt to represent people or objects from the observable world.

Academic art Art that conformed to the principles of the academies – official art schools such as the French Academy and the Royal Academy.

Acrylic Synthetic paint, now commonly used in favour of oil paint. It dries much more quickly, but does not achieve the translucent quality of oils.

Attribute An object or symbol traditionally used to identify a person or concept.

Attribution The assignment of a work of art to a particular artist, when authorship is not certain.

Bodycolor see **Gouache**

Camera obscura (Latin: "dark chamber") Camera-like apparatus used to project an image onto a screen so that outlines can be traced.

Chiaroscuro (Italian: "light dark") The effects of light and shadow in a painting, particularly when they contrast dramatically.

Complementary color Two colors are complementary if they combine to complete the spectrum. Red/green, yellow/violet, and blue/orange are the basic pairs. Placed next to each other, both appear more vibrant.

Cool and warm colors The more blue a color contains, the cooler it is. Cool colors appear to recede; warm colors, containing larger amounts of red, appear to advance.

Craquelure Fine cracks that appear on the surface of a painting as a result of aging and drying of paint.

Fresco Method of wall painting in which powdered pigments mixed with lime water are applied to fresh, wet plaster, with which they bond. This is *buon fresco*, true fresco. In *fresco secco*, or dry fresco, paint is applied to dry plaster and is susceptible to flaking.

Genre Category of painting – history painting, for example.

Genre painting Paintings depicting scenes from daily life.

Gouache Opaque watercolor paint. Also known as bodycolor.

Tondo

History painting Paintings depicting biblical, literary, mythological, or historical scenes, intended to be morally uplifting.

Impasto Thickly applied paint.

Medium Material – oil paint or pastel, for example – in which a work is executed. Also the substance (oil, egg yolk, water) which is mixed with pigment to make paint.

Oil painting Painting in which oils such as linseed, walnut, or poppy are used as the medium.

Perspective Method of representing the illusion of spatial recession on a flat surface. Linear perspective echoes the optical phenomena whereby objects appear smaller, and parallel lines converge with increasing distance. Aerial perspective mimics the effect whereby far distant objects appear pale and blue.

Picture plane The plane in which a painting's imaginary space is occupied by the actual surface of the picture.

Predella A row of small paintings set below the main panels of an altarpiece.

Renaissance A period of artistic and intellectual "rebirth" that developed in Europe from the 14th to 16th century.

Tempera Term used to refer to tempera painting, in which pigments are often bound with egg.

Tondo A circular painting.

Tone Lightness or darkness of a colour on a scale from black to white.

Trompe l'oeil (French: "deceives the eye") Painting (or part of one) intended to trick the spectator into thinking it is a real object.

Vanishing point In paintings using linear perspective, the point on the horizon at which converging lines meet.

Watercolor Paintings in which pigments, bound with water-soluble gum arabic, are applied in thinned, translucent washes.

Workshop The artist's studio and the apprentices andtrained artists who worked there with the master.

Symbols

Here is a list to help you recognize some of the symbols you may see in Western art.

Ape Vice and lust. Also a symbol of painting and sculpture.
Apple Fall of man and his redemption through Christ.
Bird Human soul.
Bubbles Life's brevity.
Butterfly Human soul.
Candle Life's brevity. Also all-seeing God.
Cherry Heaven.
Clock Time passing.
Dog Envy and lust. In portraiture: fidelity.
Dove Holy Spirit, peace. As attribute of Venus: love and lust.
Egg Creation, rebirth, Resurrection. Ostrich egg, the Virgin birth.
Fish Christ; Christianity.
Flag White with red cross; banner of the Resurrection.
Garden In Christian art, a walled garden symbolizes Mary's virginity.
Gourd Attribute of the pilgrim; symbol of the Resurrection.
Grape In Christian art: the blood of Christ.
Hare/Rabbit Lust.
Ivy Eternal life. Also an attribute of Bacchus.
Knot The ties of love.
Lamb Christ in his sacrificial role. Also innocence.
Lily Purity.
Lute With broken string, discord, death.
Palm branch In secular art: victory, fame. In Christian art: the sign of a martyr.
Peacock Attribute of Juno; in Christian art: immortality and the Resurrection.
Pelican Christ in his sacrificial role.
Pomegranate Resurrection, chastity, the authority of the Church or the monarch.
Scallop shell Attribute of Venus; sign of the pilgrim.
Skull Death.
Snake The Devil; Original Sin; sex ; the life force.
Tree Life's union of heaven and earth; the Cross; renewal, rebirth.
Wheel Fortune's wheel; fate; the round of existence; attribute of St. Catherine.

Scallop shell

Gods and goddesses

The Romans assimilated the deities of ancient Greece but gave them Latin names. Here are a few of those you might see in paintings (Greek names in brackets).

Venus and Cupid

Apollo (Apollo) The sun god, and god of reason, archery, and poetry is shown as a beautiful youth, often wearing a crown of laurel leaves, driving a four-horse chariot.
Bacchus (Dionysus) God of wine and fertility, he is usually shown as a naked youth with a crown of vine leaves and grapes, sometimes on a triumphal chariot.
Cupid (Eros) The god of love is shown as a pretty, winged youth, sometimes blindfolded; he often has a bow, arrow, and quiver.
Diana (Artemis) The moon goddess and personification of chastity is shown as a virgin huntress, accompanied by dogs or a stag. She wears a crescent moon on her brow.
Hercules (Heracles) Not a god, but the personification of strength and courage. Often wears lion's skin and carries a club.
Juno (Hera) Wife of Jupiter, protectress of women and child-birth. Usually shown with a peacock.
Jupiter (Zeus) Supreme ruler of gods and mortals; attributes include the eagle and a thunderbolt.
Mars (Ares) The destructive god of war, mostly shown in art when tamed by Venus.
Mercury (Hermes) Messenger of the gods; youthful, athletic figure with winged sandals, a hat, and a magic wand entwined with snakes.
Minerva (Pallas Athena) Virgin goddess of wisdom, originally of war for just causes, she wears armor; often accompanied by an owl.
Neptune (Poseidon) God of the sea, shown as an old man with long hair, carries a trident (three-pronged fork).
Saturn (Cronus) God of agriculture and time, he carries a scythe.
Venus (Aphrodite) Goddess of love and fertility. She has many attributes including doves or swans, a scallop shell, a magic girdle, and a flaming torch. Often accompanied by Cupid and the Three Graces.
Vulcan (Hephaestus) God of fire, depicted as a crippled blacksmith.

Saints

Here is a list of Christian saints you may come across in Western art.

St. Andrew The apostle, patron saint of Scotland and Greece, usually shown as an old man with a white beard, carrying an X-shaped cross.

St. Anne Mother of the Virgin Mary; usually shown wearing a green cloak (symbol of spring, rebirth, and immortality) over a red robe (symbol of love).

St. Catherine of Alexandria Her attributes are a wheel (on which she was tortured), a palm (sign of a martyr), and a ring (alluding to her mystic marriage to Christ).

St. Francis of Assisi He is recognizable by his brown or gray friar's habit tied with a girdle of three knots (representing the vows of poverty, chastity, and obedience), and by his stigmata (wounds corresponding to those of the crucified Christ).

St. George Warrior saint and martyr, shown in armor on a white horse slaying a dragon. He carries a shield or a flag with a cross.

St. Jerome His usual attributes are his red cardinal's hat and a lion.

St. John the Baptist The messenger of Christ, shown as an adult, dressed in animal skin,he almost always carries a reed cross with a long, slender stem.

St. John the Evangelist Apostle and one of the four evangelists (Matthew, Mark, Luke, and John); his attributes are a book or scroll, a chalice with a snake (he survived a poisoned cup), and a cauldron (he survived being thrown into a cauldron of boiling oil).

St. George and the Dragon

St. Joseph Husband of the Virgin Mary, Joseph's attributes are a lily (chastity), carpenter's tools, and a flowering rod or wand.

St. Jude Apostle, martyr, and patron saint of lost causes, Jude's attributes are a club, halberd (a type of ax), or lance, all of which refer to different accounts of his death.

St. Luke Evangelist, and patron saint of painters, Luke's attribute is an ox.

St. Mark This evangelist's attribute is the winged lion.

St. Matthew Apostle, and traditionally the author of the first gospel, Matthew is usually shown with a winged figure, which may be dictating as Matthew writes.

St. Michael The archangel Michael is usually shown in armour, along with Satan in semi-human form, or as a dragon, about to be slain by the saint.

St. Peter Martyr Dominican friar and martyr, shown in friar's habit, usually with a sword, knife, or hatchet in his skull.

St. Thomas The apostle "doubting Thomas" has various attributes: a builder's set square or rule (he is the patron of architects); the girdle (thrown down to him by the Virgin to prove she had ascended into heaven); and the spear or dagger (the instrument of his martyrdom).

St. Thomas Becket Archbishop of Canterbury and martyr; dressed in episcopal robes or black habit under red vestment. May have a sword embedded in his skull.

St. Sebastian Saint and martyr, usually shown naked and pierced with arrows.

Paintings on display

The following is a list of galleries and museums that exhibit the paintings reproduced in this book. Unless otherwise stated, all paintings in this book are oil on canvas.

Key: t = top b = bottom c = center l = left r = right

KM: Kunsthistorisches Museum, Vienna; **MO:** Musée d'Orsay, Paris; **NG:** National Gallery, London; **NGW:** National Gallery of Art, Washington; **TG:** Tate Gallery, London; **UF:** Uffizi, Florence; **V&A:** Victoria and Albert Museum, London.

Blue and Silver – Old Battersea Bridge, *Whistler*

p. 6 br: *Madonna and Child with Saints*, Piero della Francesca, Brera Gallery, Milan.
p. 7 bl: *Double Portrait of Federico da Montefeltro and Battista Sforza*, UF.
p. 8 bl: *The Ascension of St. John the Baptist with Saints, St. Gabriel*, Giovanni del Ponte, br: *The Adoration of the Kings*, Botticelli, NG.
pp. 8–9 t: *Burial at Ornans*, Courbet, MO.
p. 9 bl: *Miniature of Alice Hilliard*, Hilliard, V&A; br: *Morning Glory with Black*, Georgia O'Keeffe, The Cleveland Museum of Art.
p. 10 tr: *St. George and the Dragon*, Tintoretto, NG; bl: *Joachim Banished from the Temple*, Giotto, Arena Chapel, Padua.
p. 11 tl: *Seaport with the Embarkation of the Queen of Sheba*, Claude, NG; tr: *The Death of Marat*, David, Musées Royaux des Beaux-Arts de Belgique, Brussels; bl: *Blue and Silver – Old Battersea Bridge*, Whistler, Hunterian Art Gallery, University of Glasgow.
p. 12 cr: *Bacchus and Ariadne*, Titian, NG.
p.13 tl: *Yellow Landscape*, Roderic O'Conor, TG; tr: *Mrs. St. John Hutchinson*, Vanessa Bell, cl: *Young Woman Holding a Black Cat*, Gwen John, TG.
p. 14 bl: *Composition with Red, Yellow, and Blue*, Mondrian, TG.
p. 15 t: *The Adoration of the Golden Calf*, Poussin, NG.
p. 16 tr: *Martyrdom of St. Sebastian*, Pollaiuolo, NG; bl: *Hunters in the Snow*, Bruegel, KM.
p. 17 tl; *The Château de Steen (Autumn Landscape with View of Het Steen in the Early Morning)*, Rubens, NG; cl: *A Boy Bringing Pomegranates*, Pieter de Hooch, Wallace Collection, London; br: *Yacht Approaching the Coast*, Turner, TG.
p. 18 tl: *The Virgin and Child with Sts. Jerome and Sebastian*, Crivelli, NG; bl: *A Young Woman Standing at a Virginal*, Vermeer, NG.
p. 19 tl: *Clarinet and Bottle of Rum on a Mantlepiece*, Braque, TG, tr: *Euclidian Walks*, Magritte, Minneapolis Institute of Art; b: *Cossacks*, Kandinsky, TG.
p. 20 tr: *The Mocking of Christ*, Fra Angelico, Museo di San Marco, Florence; bl: *Last Supper*, Leonardo, Sta. Maria delle Grazie, Milan.
p. 21 tl: *An Allegory with Venus and Time*, Tiepolo, br: *The Incredulity of St. Thomas*, Cima, NG.
p. 22 tr: *The Virgin and Child*, Duccio, NG.
p. 23 tr: *Portrait of a Man*, Antonello da Messina, NG; cl: *The Morning Walk*, Gainsborough, NG; br: *In the Garden at Bougival*, Morisot, National Museum of Wales.
p. 24 cl: *Lake Lucerne*, Turner, TG.
p. 25 tl: *The Pipe Bearer*, Lewis, Cecil Higgins Art Gallery, Bedford, England.
p. 26 tr: *A Poulterer's Shop*, Dou, NG; cl: *The Laughing Cavalier*, Hals, Wallace Collection, London.
p. 27 bl: *Man in a Turban*, Van Eyck, NG.
p. 28 bl: *The Oath of the Horatii*, David, Louvre, Paris.
pp. 28–29 bl: *Guernica*, Picasso, Cason del Buen Retiro, Madrid.
p. 29 tl: *Portrait of a Lady in Yellow*, Baldovinetti, NG; cr: *Hoarfrost*, Pissarro, MO; br: *The Brioche*, Chardin, Louvre, Paris.
p. 30 cl: *St. Francis Bears Witness to the Christian Faith before the Sultan*, Sassetta, NG; cr: *The Legend of the Wolf of Gubbio*, Sassetta, NG; bl: *A Miracle of Agostino Novello*, Martini, Museo dell'Opera Metropolitana, Siena.
p. 31 tl: *Fall of Icarus*, Bruegel, Musées Royaux des Beaux-Arts de Belgique, Brussels; cr: *The Resurrection of the Soldiers*, Stanley Spencer, Sandham Memorial Chapel, Burghclere, Hants, England; b: *Whaam!*, Roy Lichtenstein, TG.
p. 32 c: *The Supper at Emmaus*, Caravaggio, NG.
p. 33 tl: *Judith Beheading Holofernes*, Gentileschi, UF.
p. 34–35 *Marriage à la Mode series*, Hogarth, NG.
p. 36 tr: *The Crucifixion with the Virgin, Sts. John, Jerome, and Mary Magdalene*, Perugino, NGW; bl: *The Small Crucifixion*, Grünewald, NGW.
p. 37 t: *The Creation of Adam*, Michelangelo, Vatican, Rome; br: *Adam*, Newman, TG.
p. 40 r: *Jupiter and Io*, Correggio, KM; bl: *Apollo and Daphne*, Pollaiuolo, NG; br: *Landscape with Echo and Narcissus*, Claude, NG.
p. 41 t: *Metamorphosis of Narcissus*, Dali, TG; bl: *Rape of Helen by Paris*, Follower of Fra Angelico, NG; br: *Ulysses Deriding Polyphemus*, Turner, NG.
p. 42 cr: *Minerva Chasing the Vices in the Garden of Virtue*, Mantegna, Louvre, Paris.
p. 43 tr: *An Allegory with Venus and Cupid*, Bronzino, NG.
p. 44 br: *The Gresley Jewel*, Hilliard, V&A; bl: *Equestrian Portrait of Charles I*, Van Dyck, NGL; br: *Portrait of Innocent X*, Velázquez, Galleria Doria Pamphilj, Rome.
p. 45 tr: *Self-Portrait*, Rembrandt, Kenwood House, London; bc: *General Sir Banastre Tarleton*, Reynolds, NG; br: *Girl in Profile*, Gwen John, National Museum of Wales.

Judith Beheading Holofernes, *Gentileschi*

p. 46 br: *Anne, Countess of Albemarle*, Reynolds, NG.
p. 47 tl: *Mr. and Mrs. Clark and Percy*, Hockney, TG.
p. 48 tr: *Crucifix*, Style of Segna, NG; bl: *Cupid Complaining to Venus*, Cranach, NG; br: *Paris Awards the Golden Apple to Venus*, Rubens, NG.
p. 49 c: *La Grande Odalisque*, Ingres, Louvre, Paris; b: *Nude Woman with Necklace*, Picasso, TG.
p. 50 cr: *Landscape with a Ruined Castle and a Church*, Ruisdael, NG; bl: *Cornard Wood*, Gainsborough, NG.
p. 51 tr: *Dedham from Langham*, Constable, TG; cr: *Mont Sainte-Victoire*, Cézanne, Philadelphia Museum of Art; bl: *The Cross in the Mountain*, Friedrich, Gemäldegalerie, Dresden.
p. 52 tr: *Flowers in a Terracotta Vase*, Van Huijsum, NG; br: *Still Life: An Allegory of the Vanities of Human Life*, Steenwyck, NG.
p. 53 t: *Apples and Oranges*, Cézanne, MO; br: *The Goldfish*, Matisse, Pushkin Museum, Moscow.
p. 54 bl: *The Abbé Scaglia Adoring the Virgin and Child*, Van Dyck, NG.
p. 55 tl: *Baptism of Christ*, Verrocchio, UF; bc: *A Woman*, Ascribed to Campin, NG.
p. 56 br: *Girl Leaning on a Windowsill*, Rembrandt, Dulwich Art Gallery, London; bc: *Girl at a Half-Open Door*, Rembrandt, The Art Institute of Chicago.
p. 57 tl: *Old Man with a Boy*, Robusti, KM; tr: *The Happy Couple*, Leyster, Louvre, Paris; bc: *Christ in the House of Martha and Mary*, National Gallery of Scotland, Edinburgh; br: *Last Supper at Emmaus*, Van Meegeren, Museum Boymans Van Beuningen, Rotterdam.
p. 60 tr: *Mona Lisa*, Leonardo, Louvre, Paris; c: *Rinaldo and Armida*, Kauffmann, Kenwood House, London; br: *Replica of L.H.O.O.Q.*, Duchamp, Philadelphia Museum of Art.
p. 61 *The White Horse*, Gauguin, MO; br: *The Hay Wain*, Constable, NG.

Index

Acknowledgments

PICTURE CREDITS
Every effort has been made to trace the copyright holders and we apologize in advance for any unintentional omissions. We would be pleased to insert the appropriate acknowledgment in any subsequent edition of this publication.

Key:
t: top *b*: bottom *c*: center *l*: left *r*: right

Abbreviations:
BAL: Bridgeman Art Library, London; **HA**: Hunterian Art Gallery, University of Glasgow; **KM**: Kunsthistorisches Museum, Vienna; **ML:** Musée du Louvre, Paris; **MO:** Musée d'Orsay, Paris; **NG:** Reproduced by courtesy of the Trustees, The National Gallery, London; **RMN**: Réunion des Musées Nationaux, Paris; **SC:** Scala; **TG:** Tate Gallery, London; **UF:** Uffizi Gallery, Florence; **WA:** Reproduced by permission of the Trustees, The Wallace Collection, London; **V&A:** Courtesy of the Board of Trustees of the Victoria & Albert Museum, London

Front cover: Clockwise from top left: © HA, Birnie Philip Gift; V&A; NG; NG; ML/RMN; MO/Giraudon/ BAL; NG; NG; *c*: Kenwood House/ © English Heritage
Back cover: Clockwise from top left: NG (also *tcl*); KM; Musées Royaux des Beaux-Arts de Belgique, Brussels/Giraudon/BAL; *Cupid Complaining to Venus* (detail), NG; *Madonna and Child with Saints* (detail), Brera Gallery, Milan/SC (also *c*, *cl*); V&A; *bl*, *bc* (detail), WA
Inside front flap: *t*: *A Miracle of Agostino Novello (detail)*, Museo dell'Opera Metropolitana, Siena/ SC; *b*: Courtauld Institute Galleries, London

p1: NG **p2:** *tl, tr, c (detail), cr, bl, bc*: NG; *br*: Philadelphia Museum of Art: George W. Elkins Collection **p3:** *cl*: V&A; *c, cr, br*: NG; *bl*: KM **p4:** *t, cl (detail)*: NG; *tr*: MO/RMN; *br, b, cr (detail)*: NG **p5:** TG **p6:** *bl*: after Millard Meiss **pp6-7:** *br, t (details)*: Brera Gallery, Milan/SC **p7:** *b*: UF/SC **p8:** *bl, br*: NG **pp8-9:** MO/RMN **p9:** *bl*: V&A; *br*: The Cleveland Museum of Art, Bequest of Leonard C. Hanna, Jr., 58.42/ © 1993 The Georgia O'Keeffe Foundation/ARS, New York **p10:** *tr, br*: NG; *cl*: Arena Chapel, Padua/SC **p11:** *tl*: NG; *tr*: Musées Royaux des Beaux-Arts de Belgique, Brussels/ Giraudon/ BAL; *bl*: © HA, Birnie Philip Bequest; *br*: Trustees of the British Museum, London **p12:** NG **p13:** *tl, cl*: TG; *tr, br (detail)*: TG/ © Angelica Garnett; *bl*: Courtesy of The Estate of Morris Louis and the André Emmerich Gallery, New York **p14:** *bl*: TG **p15:** NG **p16:** *tr, c*: NG; *bl, br*: KM **p17:** *tl, cr (detail)*: NG; *cl*: WA/ BAL; *br*: TG **p18:** *tl (detail)*: *The Madonna della Rondine*, Crivelli, NG; *bl*: NG **p19:** *tl, b*: TG/ © ADAGP, Paris and DACS, London, 1994; *tr*: The Minneapolis Institute of Arts, The William Hood Dunwoody Fund/ © ADAGP, Paris and DACS, London 1994 **p20:** *tr, cl (details)*: Museo di San Marco, Florence/ SC; *cr*: S. Marco, Florence/ SC; *bl*: Sta. Maria delle Grazie, Milan **p21:** *tl, bc, br*: NG; *tr*: Courtauld Institute Galleries, London **p22:** *tr, br (detail)*: NG; *cl*: Arena Chapel, Padua/ SC **p23:** *tr, tl (detail), cl, bl (detail)*: NG; *br*: National Museum of Wales **p24:** *tr*: © HA, Birnie Philip Gift; *cl*: TG; *br*: The Royal Collection © 1994 Her Majesty Queen Elizabeth II **p25:** *tl, tr (detail)*: The Trustees, The Cecil Higgins Art Gallery, Bedford; *bl*: V&A/BAL; *br, cr (detail)*: MO **p26:** *tr (detail)*: *A Poulterer's Shop*, Gerard Dou, NG; *cl (detail)*: *The Laughing Cavalier*, Frans Hals, WA; *br (detail)*: *Yellow Landscape*, Roderic O'Conor, TG **p27:** *tl (detail)*: *Aleph*, Morris Louis, Courtesy of The Estate of Morris Louis and the André Emmerich Gallery, New York; *tr, br (detail)*: *The Incredulity of of Saint Thomas*, Cima, NG; *bl (detail)*: *Man in a Turban*, Van Eyck, NG **p28:** *tr*: Royal Academy of Arts Library, London; *bl*: ML **pp28-29:** *b*: Cason del Buen Retiro, Madrid/ Artothek/ © DACS 1994 **p29:** *tl, tr*; *cr*: MO/ RMN; *br*: ML/ RMN **p30:** *cl, cr, tr (detail)*: NG; *bl*: Museo dell'Opera Metropolitana, Siena/ SC **p31:** *tl, tr (detail)*: Musées Royaux des Beaux-Arts de Belgique, Brussels/ BAL; *cl*: Scrovegni Chapel, Padua/ SC; *cr*: Sandham Memorial Chapel, Hampshire/ National Trust Photographic Library, Photo: A. C. Cooper/ © Estate of Stanley Spencer 1994, All Rights Reserved DACS; *b*: TG/ © Roy Lichtenstein/ DACS 1994 **p32:** *c, tr, bl (details)*: NG **p33:** *tl, tr, cr, bc (details)* UF/ SC **pp34-35:** NG **p36:** *tr, c (detail)*: © 1994 National Gallery of Art, Washington, Andrew W. Mellon Collection; *bl, br (detail)*: © 1994 National Gallery of Art, Washington, Samuel H. Kress Collection **p37:** *t, cl (detail)*: © Nippon Television Network Corporation 1994; *br*: TG/ Reproduced courtesy of Annalee Newman insofar as her rights are concerned **pp38-39:** NG **p40:** *tl*: By permission of the British Library; *r*: KM; *bl, br*: NG **p41:** *t*: TG/ © DEMART PRO ARTE BV/ DACS 1994; *bl, br*: NG **p42:** *tr (detail) An Allegory with Venus and Cupid*, Bronzino, NG; *cr, bl, br (details)*: ML/ RMN **p43:** NG **p44:** *tr*: V&A; *bl*: NG; *br*: Galleria Doria Pamphilj, Rome/ SC **p45:** *cl*: WA; *tr*: Kenwood House/ © English Heritage; *bl*: Ny Carlsberg Glyptotek, Copenhagen; *bc*: NG; *br*: National Museum of Wales **p46:** *tr, bl*: V&A; *br*: NG **p47:** *t*: TG/ © David Hockney 1970-71; *cl*: Design Museum, London; *bc, br*: TG Archive, London **p48:** *tl, bl, br*: NG **p49:** *tl*: The Royal Collection © 1994 Her Majesty Queen Elizabeth II; *tr*: NG; *c*: ML/ RMN; *b*: TG/ © DACS 1994 **p50:** *tc (detail)*: *Apollo and Daphne*, Pollaiuolo, NG; *tr (detail)*: *The Martyrdom of Saint Sebastian*, Pollaiuolo, NG; *cr, bl*: NG **p51:** *tr*: TG; *cl*: Archiv für Kunst und Geschichte, Berlin; *cr*: Philadelphia Museum of Art, George W. Elkins Collection **p52:** *cl (detail)*: *The Supper at Emmaus*, Caravaggio, NG; *tr, c (detail), br, bl (detail)*: NG **p53:** *t, bl*: MO/ Giraudon/ BAL; *br*: Pushkin Museum, Moscow/ Artothek/ © Succession H. Matisse/ DACS 1994 **p54:** *tl (detail)*: *The Madonna della Rondine*, Crivelli, *tl, bl, b*, NG **p55:** *tl, cr (detail)*: UF/ SC; *bc*: NG; *br (detail)*: *Cupid Complaining to Venus*, Cranach, NG **p56:** *tr*: Dulwich Art Gallery/ BAL; *bc, br (detail)*: The Art Institute of Chicago/ Visual Arts Library, London **p57:** *tl*: KM; *tr*: ML/ RMN; *bc*: National Gallery of Scotland, Edinburgh; *br*: Museum Boymans Van Beuningen, Rotterdam **pp58-59:** Corbally Stourton Contemporary Art Ltd **p60:** *tr*: ML; *c*: Kenwood House/ © English Heritage; *bl*: V&A; *br*: Philadelphia Museum of Art, Louise and Walter Arensberg Collection/ © ADAGP, Paris and DACS, London 1994 **p61:** *tr*: MO; *cl, br*: NG **p62:** *tc*: NG; *br (detail)*: *The Supper at Emmaus*, Caravaggio, NG; *bl*: *An Allegory of Venus and Cupid*, Bronzino, NG **p63:** *tc*: NG; *bl*: © HA; *br*: UF/ SC

Additional Photography
Philippe Sebert: **p25:** *br*; **p28:** *bl*; **p58:** *tr*; **p60:** *tr* Alison Harris: **p51:** *br*; **p61:** *tr*

Loan of Materials:
Paperchase, Tottenham Court Road, London: **p14:** *tr* Hamleys, London: **p.14:** *cr* Arthur Middleton: **p22:** *bl*

Dorling Kindersley would like to thank:
Jan Green and Erica Langmuir at the National Gallery, London; Philip Steadman and Frank Brown for the computer reconstruction **p. 18.** Jo Walton and Job Rabkin for additional picture research; Hilary Bird for the index.

Author's acknowledgments:
As usual, thanks go to Ian Chilvers for the invaluable extended loans from the library. Thanks also to Robin Simon, both for his inspirational teaching in the past, and for the helpful discussion we had when I was planning this book. I'd also like to thank the artist Michael Nelson Tjakamarra and Corbally Stourton Contemporary Art Ltd for their help with *Kangaroo Dreaming*. Thanks also to Sue Mutimear for her comments. The *Eyewitness Art* team deserves a special mention, particularly Gwen Edmonds, Phil Hunt, Mark Johnson Davies, and Peter Jones. Finally, I'd like to thank David Edgar, with whom I most enjoy looking at paintings, for all his support and encouragement. I dedicate this book to him, with my love.